WITHDRAWN

Global Spices for Everyday Cooking

Picture credits

Ariane Bille: pp. 31, 65
BESH: p. 99 bottom
Fotolia: p. 5 all, 8, 11, 13, 18 both, 21 both, 22 both, 25 both, 26 both, 29, 36, 48 top, 51 both, 52 bottom, 66, 68 both, 71 both, 72 both, 75 both, 76 both, 92 both, 95 both, 96 bottom, 99 top, 100 both, 103, 120, 122, 123, 124, 125, 126
Kornelia Bille: pp. 16, 32, 35, 38, 41, 45 top, 46, 56, 59, 60, 80, 84, 88, 130
Sarah Golbaz: p. 7, 45 bottom, 55, 79, 105, 117, 133, 138
Shutterstock: U1, U4, pp. 37, 127
Stockfood: pp. 42, 83, 87, 90, 102, 106, 109, 110, 113, 114, 118, 137, 141, 142
Bildagentur Look: p. 48 bottom, 52 top
Wikipedia: p. 96 top

Abbreviations and Quantities

1 oz = 1 ounce = 28 grams
1 lb = 1 pound = 16 ounces 1
1 cup = approx. 5–8 ounces* (see below)
1 cup = 8 fl uid ounces = 250 milliliters (liquids)
2 cups = 1 pint (liquids) = 15 milliliters (liquids)
8 pints = 4 quarts = 1 gallon (liquids)
1 g = 1 gram = 1/1000 kilogram = 5 ml (liquids)
1 kg = 1 kilogram = 1000 grams = 2¼ lb
1 l = 1 liter = 1000 milliliters (ml) = 1 quart
125 milliliters (ml) = approx. 8 tablespoons = ½ cup
1 tbsp = 1 level tablespoon = 15–20 g* (depending on density) = 15 milliliters (liquids)
1 tsp = 1 level teaspoon = 3–5 g * (depending on density) = 5 ml (liquids)

*The weight of dry ingredients varies significantly depending on the density factor, e.g. 1 cup of flour weighs less than 1 cup of butter. Quantities in ingredients have been rounded up or down for convenience, where appropriate. Metric conversions may therefore not correspond exactly. It is important to use either American or metric measurements within a recipe.

© Verlags- und Vertriebsgesellschaft Dort- Hagenhausen Verlag- GmbH & Co. KG, Munich, Germany
Original Title: *Kochen mit ökologischen Naturgewürzen. Ein Feuerwerk der Aromen*
ISBN 978-3-86362-044-8

Recipes: Sarah Golbaz
Profiles: Hellmut Wagner
Further contributions: Christine Paxmann (pp. 9, 12, 14, 17, 47, 67, 91, 121), Gewürzkampagne UG (pp. 10, 14, 37, 126)
Project coordinators: Marcus Reckewitz, Lars Pietzschmann

Disclaimer

The information and recipes printed in this book are provided to the best of our knowledge and belief and based on our own experience, but they are not a substitute for personal consultation, examination, diagnosis, or treatment from a doctor, in particular with regard to interactions with medicines that you may be taking, and in relation to age, allergies, pregnancy, or breastfeeding. Please ensure that all plants, in particular those with a potent effect, are always used in exactly the amounts stated. The information and recipes contained in this book are used at the reader's own risk. We assume no liability for the accuracy or completeness of this information, or for any effects or adverse reactions that may occur. Neither the author nor the publisher shall accept liability for any damage whatsoever which may arise directly or indirectly from the use of this book.
This disclaimer applies in particular to the use and consumption of untreated raw milk and/or raw milk products, which the author and publisher strongly advise against due to the associated health risks. It is advisable not to serve dishes that contain raw eggs to very young children, pregnant women, elderly people, or to anyone weakened by serious illness. If in any doubt, consult your doctor. Be sure that all the eggs you use are as fresh as possible.

© for this English edition: h.f.ullmann publishing GmbH
Translation from German: Maisie Fitzpatrick in association with First Edition Translations Ltd, Cambridge, UK
Typesetting: The Write Idea, Cambridge, UK
Cover design and layout: Simone Speth, Potsdam

Overall responsibility for production: h.f.ullmann publishing GmbH, Potsdam, Germany

Printed in Germany, 2016

ISBN 978-3-8480-0934-3

10 9 8 7 6 5 4 3 2 1
X IX VIII VII VI V IV III II I

www.ullmann-publishing.com
newsletter@ullmann-publishing.com
facebook.com/hfullmann
twitter.com/hfullmann_int

SARAH GOLBAZ & HELLMUT WAGNER

Global Spices for Everyday Cooking

h.f.ullmann

Contents

Preface   6

Spicecraft   9

Today's Spices: Modern Classics   10
The Spice Route   12
Basic Facts   14

Powerful and Dynamic:
Earthy Spices   17

Profiles   18
Spotlight on Pepper   28
Recipes   30
Spotlight on Paprika   36
Spotlight on Cinnamon: "Brown Gold"   37
Recipes   39

Fragrant and Delicate:
Floral Spices   47

Profiles   48
Recipes   54

Spices with Staying Power:
Balsamic Flavors   67

Profiles   69
Recipes   78

Spices with Spirit and Sass:
The Hot Ones   91

Profiles   93
Spotlight on Mustard: A Gift from the Romans   102
Spotlight on Salt   103
Recipes   104

Exquisite, Finely Tuned Mixtures:
The Big Hitters   121

Homemade Spice Mixtures   122
Spotlight on Spice Mixtures   126
Spotlight on Curry Powder   127
Recipes   128

Index of Recipes   144

Preface

Enjoying delicious food is my great pleasure in life. No doubt this is because I have been around people who love cooking ever since I was little. Of course, there is also the fact that I love experimenting with spices and flavors. When I was a child, I would try to guess the smells that wafted through the streets at lunchtime as I ran home from school. The closer I got to my family's house, the more excited I became about what my mother would have lovingly conjured up for the midday meal.

I am half Iranian and half French—both cultures that prize hospitality. We usually had two cooked meals a day. My childhood was filled with the fragrance of Persian Basmati rice with saffron, of grilled chicken with Provençal herbs. When I smell those aromas today, I am immediately filled with a sense of contentment as I associate them with so many lovely memories of family and friends gathered round the dining table. We did not eat merely to fill ourselves up, but rather to savor the food and celebrate those precious everyday moments.

Spices play an important role in my cooking because they have the power to transform simple meals into something special. I love creating dishes that add to a sense of well-being, and I am always on the lookout for new combinations of spices that bring out and underpin the flavor of individual ingredients.

I believe that the quality of ingredients is the most important thing in cooking, rather than the quantity on the plate—my motto is "A bit of everything." When choosing spices, I look for local and good-quality organic products. Making choices like this shows an appreciation of nature, something that is important to me. Eating should make you happy, after all, and taking the "history" of the spice into consideration is part of that. Has it been grown organically and carefully harvested? Is it fairly traded? Was it cultivated and processed in harmony with nature? Once it has been processed, is the end product free of toxic substances or irritants that come through in the taste? Certain nuances in a dish that is based heavily on spices can make all the difference between a complete flop in terms of taste and a spectacular burst of flavors. The purer, fresher, and more carefully processed a spice is, the more effectively you can use it to tweak dishes and serve up food that delights body and soul.

Sarah Golbaz

Spicecraft

Spices bring the whole world into our homes. The sheer diversity of them is greater now than ever before. Transcontinental travel and cuisine have changed our palates and the way in which we experience foods that are bitter, sour, sweet, or spicy. Yet this is by no means a recent phenomenon. There is, in fact, a long tradition of using exotic spices. Pre-Christian trade routes brought spices from the East, and the Crusades created even more demand. Ultimately, however, it was explorers who really brought about a taste revolution, when they returned from their travels in India, China, South America, and Africa. Back in Europe, meanwhile, monasteries grew herbs that were used in remarkable remedies. The spice trade was on a par with that of gold or salt. Whatever tasted good was sold by the shipload, in particular spices that could pep up the somewhat bland food of the time. Proper experimentation by top chefs got under way in the 18th century, when the spice monopolies collapsed and flavors from all over the world became mass-produced goods. Today they are variously seen as mood enhancers, remedies, trend barometers, superfoods, and troves of gustatory experimentation amongst hipster chefs. First and foremost, however, spices are natural products that must be traded fairly. After all, by the time that delicious product adds its special touch to your vegetable or meat dish, it already has a long journey behind it, which needs to be founded on a careful balance between humans and nature.

Today's Spices: Modern Classics

In order to grasp the significance of spices in cooking today, we first need to take a close look at modern cooking culture. "Modern" no longer means a focus on one particular cuisine, such as Mediterranean, Asian, or Chinese, although such traditions continue to be hugely important.

Modern cooking is instead defined by a love of unfettered experimentation, which involves the fusion of different types of cuisine. We have relatively few inhibitions about borrowing from different traditions; instead, we simply see what goes together, which ingredients enhance each other's flavors, and which do not (because not everything works in a pairing, not by any means). That leads to fresh and exciting new interpretations of classic regional dishes. A glance at the menus of top restaurants in the parts of big cities where things happen is enough to reveal how much this trend has caught on. There is also a newfound love of vegetarian and vegan cuisine, which itself borrows from a wide range of cooking cultures in order to fashion a new concept.

Cooking in this way means that spices become hugely important. They often provide the flagship tastes of the cuisines that are dipped into by those who like to experiment, and which are familiar for their spices more than anything. Spices give a kick to vegetarian and vegan cuisine, which eschews meat and animal fats as flavor carriers.

While a mere pinch of salt and perhaps a little caraway might suffice for a classic dish of roast pork with onions and potatoes, a hot cauliflower curry will not work without a whole range of top-quality spices. The humble cauliflower, often frowned upon by professional chefs as too pungent, needs ginger, chili powder, coriander, garam masala, cumin, and turmeric to taste its best, to name but a few. Spices and spice blends are therefore invaluable in creating exciting dishes from a few simple ingredients. Nowadays, they are the proverbial "extra something."

Versatility

Alongside their main role as flavoring agents and standard-bearers for specific culinary traditions, some spices can also make dishes more wholesome; indeed, many of them are predominantly used for their health benefits. Turmeric, the ground root of the eponymous plant, is a good example of all three aspects. Owing to its striking yellow hue and mild piquancy, it is a popular spice and thus an important ingredient in many Indian curry powders. And because turmeric also has anti-inflammatory properties, it is often used for health purposes, sometimes in large quantities.

The importance of spices in modern cooking, where traditions are borrowed with abandon, means that high-quality products are needed in order to impart an optimum flavor. Whereas previously chefs strove to use ingredients that were as exotic as possible in order to take a dish to new heights, today the emphasis is on the quality of each individual ingredient. This return to an attitude of "less is more," and "letting quality shine through," has meant that spices are now playing a more important role in cooking. Being able to pull off a great many simple modern recipes, some of them not widely known, depends entirely upon the quality of those spices.

Ideally, spices should be organically and sustainably grown. Not only will this ensure that they are free of pesticides and fungicides, but also most producers of organically grown spice plants do not feel driven to churn out vast quantities as quickly as they possibly can, but instead try to make sure that their product is as good as possible. And you can really taste the difference!

The Spice Route

Over the millennia, spices have been variously commodities, triggers for conflict, and status symbols, keeping the world on its toes. Today, when sophisticated consumers and world travelers can obtain spices at delicatessens, discount stores, or markets during their own journeys, the diverse effects of these products are sometimes forgotten. Now that spices are readily available, their appeal is mostly centered round refining dishes. But it was not always like that. For a long time, the countries where the spices that we find in our kitchen racks today were grown—such as cardamom, chili powder, nutmeg, vanilla, coriander, cloves, cinnamon, pepper, and ginger—could be reached only with extreme difficulty, and trade took place along dangerous overland routes. The Silk Road, which has existed since the Bronze Age, was the most important channel for spices transported from Asia to Europe. The market was dominated by the Phoenicians and Arabs, who carried their precious cargoes through the Middle East and Egypt to the Mediterranean region, where Constantinople, Venice, and Genoa were the most important ports. Exotic spices were popular from antiquity, as not only did they improve the taste of generally bland dishes, but they also had demonstrable curative effects. The essential oils contained in the spices promote digestion and stimulate blood circulation, and were often used to mask the bad taste of overcooked dishes or sour drinks such as wine and beer. Merchants had long brought small plants from East to West, and ambitious gardeners sought to cultivate them in Europe, despite its harsher climate. Their efforts were not always successful. By the early Middle Ages, when the land route became blocked due to conflicts such as those arising from Islamization and the Crusades, Benedictine monks had long been cultivating herb gardens, in which they grew sage, marjoram, and juniper. As far back as the 11th century, the abbess and physician Hildegard von Bingen discovered properties of nutmeg, cloves, cinnamon, ginger, and pepper that are still used to this day.

A must-have

In the past, spices were used as remedies, preservatives, flavorings, and fragrances. Marco Polo's famous account of his travels and the active trade between East and West at the time of the Crusades, between the 11th and 13th centuries, awoke a desire for such seasonings in Europe. Anyone who could afford to do so would over-spice their dishes and drinks. The mulled wine of today is but a pale imitation of the spiced booze that was prevalent in the Middle Ages. Royal houses such as those of Spain, Portugal, Italy, and the Netherlands fought over the spice-producing countries. Their financiers, rich merchants such as the Fugger family of Augsburg,

dominated the market. By the time Indian pepper reached the harbor of Venice, its value was thirty times higher because the "pepper galleys" had to be able to outrun fast clippers, driving the local price skyward. Spice merchants became exceedingly wealthy. Nutmegs, seen as status symbols and precious, aphrodisiac gifts, were strung around their owners' necks on gold chains.

In 1492 Columbus' quest for a sea route to India on behalf of Spain was driven by a lust for gold and spices. Instead he found America and with it, previously unknown foods such as chillies, vanilla, and all spice. In 1496 Vasco da Gama's discovery of that Indian sea route changed the trade overnight. Portugal became a spice monopoly until the Dutch founded the East India Trading Company in 1602, dominating the market until the18th century. On the flipside, the soil and plants from the spices' countries of origin—in particular Moluccas (Spice Islands)—were almost destroyed as they were so fought over. The aptly named Pierre Poivre ("pepper") finally ended the conflict. He smuggled cloves and nutmeg to Mauritius and other French colonies and managed to cultivate them there. East India Company collapsed, only Spain's vanilla monopoly prevailed, guarded from Mexico. This also finally fell in the early 19th century with former slave Edmund Albius managing to artificially inseminate the vanilla flower on Reunion. Prices fell and trade went global. Nowadays no country has exclusive rights to any spice and they are traded on stock exchanges worldwide.

Basic Facts

Where can you buy top-quality spices?

It is not always easy to get hold of good-quality products. Many supermarkets and discount stores offer mass-market goods only. Beware of products endorsed by TV and celebrity chefs, too. Some that bear the names of famous people may be grossly overpriced, and the labels on some disguise low-quality goods. It is well worth doing some research into what is really in the jar or package. Labels often give information about the source, and the internet may offer you more guidance on that. Of course, there are myriad good producers. Lots of health-food stores sell a wide range of spices, unusual ones as well as commonly used ones.

The quality of the spices should not be your only concern. The packaging is equally important. A substantial amount of the price may relate to the container rather than its contents, and the containers may not be in accordance with sustainability standards either. If you are watching the price, look out for spices that are imported directly, without intermediaries that drive the product price up. Look for Fair Trade goods, too. When you buy those the producers receive a good return for their efforts. With just a little effort yourself, you will secure great quality products.

It's all about the storage

Once you are satisfied that your spices are of good quality, it is important to keep them as fresh as possible after purchasing by storing them properly. Dry spices do not tend to go bad or moldy, and the expiry date shown on the label is normally far into the future. However, spices can lose their flavor and color. To avoid this, you should take care to store them in dry, light-proof, and airtight packaging or in a similar container. Packaging with a little cellophane window might look pretty, but it does not offer optimal protection against light. Small containers that are lightproof and airtight are ideal for everyday use, and can be topped up as needed. Special metal tins are good, as are brown apothecary-style jars.

Homegrown herbs

Anyone who has their own balcony or garden has the chance to grow their own herbs. It is best to buy seeds and plant them yourself, or to use plants from a nursery. Top tip: sprinkle freshly picked herbs with a little water and then freeze them loose. That way you will always have portions of fresh herbs ready to use.

Table salt	Add at any time
Fleur de sel	Do not cook with it; use it only for seasoning, so that the salt retains its structure
Pepper (black)	If necessary, heat before grinding in order to release the flavors. Do not add ground pepper to hot oil or butter, as this will make the taste bitter.
Paprika, marjoram, basil, oregano, cinnamon	These should be added at a relatively late stage, at the very earliest after the pan has been deglazed.
Thyme, rosemary, sage	These withstand heat well and can be added when frying, but should not be left to boil for long.
Cumin, mustard seeds	Release their flavors when heated, so can be added to butter or liquid, even if they have not been ground.
Saffron	Releases its flavor only slowly. Crush in a mortar first and leave to stand in a little liquid (water, vinegar, wine, or milk), before using in cooking.

How should spices be added?

Spices differ not only in appearance and flavor, but also in the way in which they should be used. For instance, rosemary and thyme withstand heat very well and can be added early on in cooking without any problem, or added to hot oil. Paprika and marjoram, however, should never be added directly to hot oil or butter, because they become bitter very quickly if heated in this way. At the very earliest, they should be added after liquid is poured into a dish, so that they can cook in the pan along with the other ingredients. Pepper, by contrast, tastes best if it is briefly toasted in a hot, dry pan before being ground, so that it can release its full flavor. Try it just once, and you will be amazed by the difference. Essentially, it is worth finding out the characters of each spice and the optimal point at which to add it to your cooking. Here are a few practical pointers for using the most common spices:

Powerful and Dynamic:

Earthy Spices

The most prominent earthy spices, including smoked paprika, long pepper, and smoked salt, are certainly not for the faint of tongue. These spices are capable of taking dishes in a whole new direction. Meanwhile, the pungent notes of cinnamon and nutmeg stimulate hormonal balance, aid metabolism, and fire up the taste buds. In terms of taste, caraway, coriander, and cumin not only add elusive or even smoky notes to food, but also promote digestibility when cooked with hearty dishes based on cabbage, meat, and pulses. With their chocolaty flavors, turmeric and coriander provide the finishing touch to dishes that combine lots of flavors, from stews to curries, and roast dinners to wintry vegetable feasts. Earthy spices are star players in the culinary concerto.

Coriander

Origins and distribution

Coriander belongs to the parsley family and takes one or two years to reach maturity. It has long been cultivated, and is originally from the Balkans and the eastern Mediterranean region. Grave finds from Egypt show that coriander has been highly prized since ancient times as a herb and a medicinal plant. Coriander is still widely used today, and is all over the world. The main suppliers, however, are North African countries such as Morocco, Tunisia, and Egypt, as well as Central and South America. The word "coriander" is thought to come from the Greek. Its root word, "koris," means "bedbug." Indeed, the typical and normally pleasant smell of coriander is, for many people, reminiscent of the odor of bedbugs. As a fresh herb, coriander is known as "cilantro" in Spanish-speaking countries and is commonly used for the leaves. This name has also caught on in other countries.

Use

Coriander is primarily used in the form of ground seeds in European and North American cuisine. In South and Central America and the Iberian peninsula it tends to be used more as a fresh herb. Cilantro has a slightly lemony, bitter, and pungent taste, while coriander seeds have a herby tang about them, and only slight bitterness. For this reason coriander seeds are a key component in many spice blends. Coriander seeds are an important ingredient in curry powders, for instance, as well as in many gingerbread and bread seasoning mixes. In order to prevent the bitter elements of the coriander seed from overpowering the overall taste, you should grind the seeds just before adding them to your cooking. Cilantro is used in cuisine in the same way as flat-leaf parsley. Do bear in mind that many people have an aversion to what they perceive as coriander's "soapy" flavor, and some have an allergic reaction to it. The aldehyde in coriander, which is very similar to that found in soaps and shampoos, can trigger a violent immune response.

Cumin

Origins and distribution

Cumin has been cultivated in North Africa, Turkey, Syria, Central America, and India for millennia, and belongs to the parsley family.
Cumin has an unmistakable earthy-sweet taste and gives lots of oriental dishes their savory note. The Turkish air-cured beef delicacy pastirma and Turkish sujuk sausage would be unthinkable with cumin. The Indian spice mix garam masala also contains a hefty helping of ground cumin.

Use

Dried cumin seeds are used either whole or in ground form. Due to its very strong—indeed, dominant—flavor, it should be used sparingly and sprinkled carefully from the jar. If it is being cooked, it is best to use seeds that have been freshly crushed in a mortar. The ground powder is ideal for seasoning. The whole seeds can also be toasted in a pan with just a little oil, so that they release their powerful nutty flavor.

Caraway

Origins and distribution

Caraway, also known as meridian fennel or Persian cumin, belongs to the parsley family. The plant takes two years to complete its life cycle. Originally, it was endemic to the lands round the Mediterranean and the Middle East. Today it is mainly cultivated in the moderate climate zones of Europe, and also in Egypt. When the seed pods are harvested, they yield up to 3.75 tons per acre (1.5 tonnes per hectare). Caraway is one of the oldest spices in human history. Excavations have uncovered caraway seeds that are about 5,000 years old. Caraway also has a long history as a medicinal plant. Adding two cups of water to a teaspoon of crushed caraway seeds and bringing the mixture to the boil has long been one of the most widespread home remedies for flatulence and stomach trouble. In the Middle Ages, sumptuous celebratory banquets were often rounded off with sweet baked goods that were heavily spiced with caraway.

Use

Caraway is a popular all-round spice in modern cooking. It is used to season boiled potatoes, for example, or included because its digestive properties work particularly well in fatty roast pork, goose, and duck dishes. Caraway is an indispensable ingredient in seasoning for sauerkraut and red and white cabbage. It also gives various spirits their distinctive flavor, including Aquavit and Köm.

Turmeric

Origins and distribution

Turmeric is a spice plant from the ginger family, and is endemic to India, Southeast Asia, and South America. A herbaceous, perennial plant, it grows up to 6 feet (2 meters) high. Its beautiful inflorescences, which range from cream colored to reddish, are also harvested as cut flowers.

Interesting fact

Turmeric is famous for its vibrant color. The rhizome (rootstock) contains large quantities of the pigment curcumin. This substance is considered to have antioxidant, cancer-inhibiting, and anti-inflammatory effects.

Use

The whole, ground, or chopped rhizome is dried and used as a spice. Turmeric is most commonly used as a key ingredient in curry powders. The use of ground turmeric on its own is less common in northern latitudes, although it offers lots of fantastic possibilities in cooking. One easy tip is to stir a generous amount of turmeric into cooking oil and spread the mixture onto chicken breast fillets. When the chicken is grilled it develops an exquisite flavor and takes on a magnificent golden hue. Adding just a pinch of turmeric to scrambled eggs gives them an amazing color and taste.

Long pepper

Origins and history

Long pepper, also known as Indian long pepper, belongs to the pepper family and is closely related to the well-known black pepper variety. Interestingly, this kind of pepper arrived in Europe long before the sort that is commonly used today. Alexander the Great is believed to have brought long pepper and other spices back to Greece from his conquering expeditions in India about 340 BC. For centuries, the Greeks and Romans imported this type of pepper from India, and it was highly prized as a spice and as a remedy. It was only in the 17th century that this kind of pepper began to be increasingly displaced by black pepper. As a result, it is now rather obscure and only rarely found in stores.

Cultivation

Long pepper has spread round the globe from its original home in India to form the "pepper belt" between the 20th parallel north and the 20th parallel south. Today it is mostly grown in India, West Africa, the Sunda Islands, the Philippines, and the Caribbean.

Use

In terms of taste, long pepper is strongly reminiscent of black pepper, but has a slightly sweetish-sour note. It may be used in the same way as black pepper. Its special flavor gives dishes an exotic touch, and it is often used in spice blends such as curry powders.

Nutmeg

Origins and history

The nutmeg tree has an impressive appearance, growing up to 60 feet (20 meters) and sporting mostly dark green, lance-shape leaves and dense branches. It originally came from the southern Moluccas. Arab sailors are thought to have brought the first nutmegs to Europe in the 6th century. In the Middle Ages nutmegs changed hands for prices that seem incredible today—a single nutmeg cost as much as half a cow. This was one of the reasons for the war that broke out in the 17th century between Portugal and the Netherlands over the Moluccas, which today belong to Indonesia. The Netherlands emerged the victor and went on to dominate the nutmeg trade until the 18th century. It was only when Pierre Poivre, a French follower of the Enlightenment and horticultural expert, succeeded in smuggling a nutmeg seed to Réunion and grew it there, that prices fell. Today nutmeg is cultivated in tropical areas north and south of the equator. One of the finest nutmeg-producing areas is on the island of Grenada, in the Antilles. Nutmegs have become the small state's main source of income, alongside tourism. The importance of this spice for Grenada is evident from the national coat of arms, which shows a ripe nutmeg cracking open.

Harvesting and cultivation

In many countries that export nutmegs, the nutmeg tree is not cultivated in plantations, but scattered through the tropical forest. A single nutmeg tree can produce up to 15,000 nuts per year. As soon as the fruit, which looks like a ripe apricot, bursts and the fiery red aril is visible, it is ready to be harvested. First the fruit pulp is removed, and the aril, which is processed to make mace, is carefully stripped away and dried separately in the sun. As soon as the seed within has been freed, the shell is broken to free the coveted nutmeg.

Use

When freshly shredded using a nutmeg grater, this highly aromatic spice can be used to enhance soups, sauces, vegetables, and meat dishes. Nutmeg is also found in certain spice blends.

Smoked paprika

Origins and history

Smoked paprika is a specialty made from the sweet fruits of the pepper plant (*Capiscum annuum*). Originally endemic to South America, paprika owes its immense popularity in Europe to Columbus, who is said to have brought the seeds of the pepper plant back to Spain from his third journey to South America in 1498–1500. The spice plant thrived in Spain, from where it spread to all European countries with a Mediterranean climate. It is cultivated extensively in southern Hungary and Serbia, in particular, as well as in other Balkan countries, and it continues to be important to the economy of certain regions to this day. Unsurprisingly, these same areas produce the most delicious smoked paprika.

Production

In the Balkans, the highly aromatic smoky flavor is produced by splitting the peppers into long strings and smoking them once they are half-dry. They get their taste from the material used to smoke them—a mixture of oak chippings and dry vine cuttings. Smoked paprika has also long been traditional in Spain, particularly in the southwest, where peppers are laid out in large, covered drying lofts and flavored with hot smoke from holm and cork oak wood. The deliciously spicy and distinctive taste of chorizo comes from the paprika powder used to make it.

Smoked salt

Production

Smoked salt, which is traditionally and predominantly used in North America, is made by flavoring coarse sea salt with smoke from hickory wood. In a process that often takes several days, salt crystals are infused with the flavor of hickory wood, which is precipitated onto it as a condensate. Of course, interesting variations on the taste can be produced by using other types of aromatic wood. Beech wood mixed with juniper twigs makes a particularly good alternative. A smoke-flavored additive is often used in modern industrial production processes.

Use

Smoked salt can be used whenever a dish can take a strong, full-flavored and smoky taste. This flavor is very much a part of North American and Tex-Mex cuisine. In Europe, too, it has long been used in stews, casseroles, potato dishes, and various sauces (e.g. for barbecued meat).

Cinnamon

Harvesting and cultivation

Cinnamon is obtained from a variety of cinnamon tree and shrub species. The cinnamon tree grows wild in the forests of Sri Lanka and can reach heights of up to 50 feet (15 meters). In plantations the tree is pruned in such a way that its shrub-like new shoots grow only to about 6 feet (2 meters). The most important varieties of cinnamon are Cassia cinnamon, also known as Chinese cinnamon, and the much finer and more aromatic Ceylon cinnamon, also described as "true cinnamon." Ceylon cinnamon sticks consist of several layers of the very finely rolled bark of shrub shoots. Chinese or Cassia cinnamon, by contrast, is obtained from shavings from the bark of the main tree. However, this bark is not completely freed from the outer layer of cork and is therefore significantly thicker than Ceylon cinnamon. It also has a harsher taste due to its higher tannin content.

Distribution

Cinnamon originates from Southeast Asia. The island of Sri Lanka is considered to be the birthplace of the cinnamon tree. Today, cinnamon is cultivated in the Caribbean, in particular on Martinique, Jamaica, and Grenada, as well as in southern India, the Seychelles, and Brazil.

Use

Cinnamon is a much-used and popular spice in our cuisine. We use it in the form of cinnamon sticks or finely ground cinnamon powder when making cakes, stewed fruit, and other sweet dishes, as well as in punch and various other hot drinks.

Note

Cassia cinnamon has particularly high coumarin levels, and is therefore considered a health risk. Cooks are advised to use only Ceylon cinnamon, which contains far less coumarin and is much more flavorsome, too.

Tonka beans

Distribution and cultivation

The natural habitat of the tonka bean tree is the Amazon region, along with Venezuela, Colombia, and Peru. It is cultivated in Nigeria, Brazil, Venezuela, and some islands of the Caribbean. The fruits that this tree produces once a year are not beans in the botanical sense, but rather seeds. These almond-shape seeds are used as a spice.

Interesting fact

Tonka beans are banned as a foodstuff in some countries owing to their high coumarin content. The consumption of more than 2 milligrams of coumarin per kilogram of food is considered dangerous. Too much coumarin can cause lasting damage to the liver and kidneys, and is also suspected to have carcinogenic effects.

Tonka beans are commonly used as lucky charms, a completely harmless custom. If worn on a necklace or carried in a purse, they are said to ensure prosperity and success in business.

Use

Due to its high coumarin content, the smell of a freshly grated tonka bean is reminiscent of aromatic hay or sweet woodruff. If used sparingly and carefully, the tonka bean is harmless and gives desserts a sweetish taste similar to that of vanilla. The beans can be shredded finely using a nutmeg grater or briefly simmered in milk or cream, which absorb their delicious, vanilla-like flavor.

Spotlight on Pepper

Pepper has been a prominent spice since time immemorial. Long pepper is first mentioned as *pippali* in Sanskrit writings from India, dating from about 1200 BC. It is thought to have originally come from the Malabar Coast of India. Indian pepper was shipped in great quantities by Arab merchants to Alexandria in Egypt, a historical trading center and pepper's first major export destination. From there, pepper was taken onward to Rome. In due course, it became the most expensive and coveted spice of all. Pepper was hugely important, even to the extent of impacting on economic policy, not only owing to its use as a spice, but also because there was no effective way of chilling fresh meat at that time, so people would use the antibacterial and preservative properties of ground pepper to cure meat. It was also useful for masking unpleasant smells. Today pepper is cultivated in plantations in sufficiently humid tropical regions near to the equator, all round the world. Pepper is a climbing shrub that is grown and cultivated on stakes or poles, similarly to the way that hops are grown. Pepper naturally grows close to tropical tree varieties that make ideal support plants. It is propagated using cuttings, and it takes three years to produce an amount that is worth harvesting. The main yield occurs between the sixth and eighth years. After about twenty years the yield is greatly reduced, so a new plantation needs to be created. Pepper can be harvested twice a year.

White, black, red, and green peppers all come from the same plant; the only difference is the point at which they are harvested. Black pepper is harvested unripe, and the drying process gives the green berries their black color and wrinkled appearance. White pepper is obtained from the mature berries, which are soaked in water after being plucked, and then lose their shell. After being dried, they take on a white to offwhite color. Green pepper is produced from the unripe berries and is dried rapidly at high temperatures. Other methods of preserving green pepper include freeze-drying it and pickling it in brine. Red pepper consists of fully ripe, gleaming red berries that are pickled in brine and thus retain their color.

Various spices that are commonly called pepper have nothing to do with real pepper, because in botanical terms they do not belong to the pepper family. The best known of these "false peppers" are pink pepper (Schinus fruit), Sichuan pepper, and Tasmanian pepper. Cayenne pepper is also a "false" pepper. It is obtained from the chili plant, which is related to the pepper family.

Key pepper varieties

Lampung pepper	from the island of Sumatra.
Malabar pepper	from the Malabar Coast of India, the birthplace of pepper.
Muntok pepper	from the Indonesian island of Banka. This pepper variety derives its name from the island's main port for shipping pepper.
Periyar pepper	from the Indian state of Kerala. Endemic varieties of pepper have long been grown extensively here, resulting in pepper with an unadulterated and complex taste.
Sarawak pepper	from the island of Borneo, which mainly produces black pepper. It is milder than the Indian varieties of pepper.
Tellicherry	from the Indian state of Kerala. This is the premium Indian pepper product and consists of hand-picked berries with a specific minimum size.

Avocado and chicken sandwich Serves 4

14 oz (400 g) chicken breast fillets
1 tbsp olive oil
¼ tsp spicy **SMOKED PAPRIKA**
1 ripe avocado
juice of 1 lemon
1 tsp **CUMIN**
1 Batavia lettuce
2 tomatoes
1 red onion
8 slices of rye bread
salt, pepper

Wash the chicken breast fillets and pat them dry. Heat the oil in a pan and fry the meat for approximately 10 minutes, turning them every so often. Season with the salt, pepper, and smoked paprika, then wrap in aluminum foil and set to one side.

Cut the avocado in half, remove the pit, scoop the fruit out of the shell with a spoon, and mash it with a fork. Add salt, lemon juice, and cumin to taste. Wash the lettuce and toss it until it is dry. Wash the tomatoes and cut them into thin slices. Peel the onion and slice it into rings. Cut the chicken breast fillets into thin slices too.

Toast the bread and spread the avocado mixture over each of the slices. Set out 4 slices of the toasted bread and lay 1 lettuce leaf, some chicken, 2 slices of tomato, onion rings, and then another lettuce leaf on each of them, before placing the second slice of bread on top. Cut the sandwiches in half and serve.

Hummus Makes approx. 1 cup (250 ml)

generous 2 cups (250 g) chickpeas
   (from a can)
1 garlic clove
3 tbsp light tahini (sesame paste)
1 tbsp olive oil
salt
2 tbsp lemon juice
1 tsp **CUMIN**

Drain the chickpeas and rinse under cold water. Peel the garlic and crush it or chop it very finely.

Blend the chickpeas to a creamy paste with the tahini, olive oil, salt, garlic, and lemon juice, using a handheld blender. Add 2 to 4 tablespoons of water if required. Add salt and cumin to taste.

Serve fresh flatbreads or vegetable crudités with the hummus.

Eggplant mousse

3 eggplants
2 garlic cloves
3 tbsp tahini (sesame paste)
juice of 2 lemons
2 tbsp olive oil + olive oil for brushing
¼ tsp **SMOKED PAPRIKA**
1 tbsp pomegranate seeds to decorate
chopped parsley to decorate
salt

Pre-heat the oven to 430 °F (220 °C). Slice the eggplants in half lengthways and score them in a crisscross pattern. Brush with a little olive oil and sprinkle with salt. Place them on a tray covered in baking parchment and bake in the oven for approximately 15 to 20 minutes. They are ready when the eggplant is soft. Remove the eggplants from the oven, scoop the flesh out with a spoon, and leave to drain in a sieve.

Peel the garlic cloves and crush them or chop them finely. Place the garlic, eggplant pieces, tahini, lemon juice, and olive oil in a bowl and mash with a fork. Add salt and paprika to taste. Garnish with the pomegranate seeds and parsley.

Caraway and thyme crispbreads

Mix the flours and yeast together. Knead for about 10 to 15 minutes with 9 tablespoons (140 ml) water and the oil to form a smooth dough. Cover with a cloth and leave to prove in a warm place for 30 minutes.

Place a baking tray in the oven and pre-heat to 410 °F (210 °C). Roll the dough out as thinly as possible on a floured surface and sprinkle with the caraway, thyme, and salt. Divide into two portions and bake in the oven for 5 to 7 minutes.

1¼ cups (180 g) wheat flour
⅔ cup (100 g) rye flour
4 g dried yeast
¼ cup (60 ml) olive oil
½ tsp **CARAWAY**
½ tsp thyme
fleur de sel for sprinkling

Potato rösti with salmon tartare Serves 4

To make the rösti, peel the potatoes and grate them roughly. Season with salt, pepper, and nutmeg and leave to stand for 3 to 4 minutes, before squeezing out thoroughly.

Heat the clarified butter in an iron pan over high heat, scatter the grated potato over the bottom of the pan and press down firmly. Fry for 10 to 12 minutes over medium heat. Turn the rösti over using the lid of a pot or a plate and fry for another 10 to 12 minutes until it is done.

Meanwhile, make the tartare. Cut the salmon into small pieces. Chop the dill finely and slice the chives into short lengths.

Mix the crème fraîche with the mustard and lemon juice, and add salt and pepper to taste.

Combine the salmon tartare with the herbs. Carefully fold in the crème fraîche. Season to taste with salt and pepper. Serve the tartare on the röstis.

For the rösti
1¼ lb (600 g) mostly waxy potatoes grated **NUTMEG**
4 tbsp clarified butter
salt, pepper

For the tartare
generous 1 lb (500 g) fresh salmon
½ bunch of dill
½ bunch of chives
6 tbsp (100 g) crème fraîche
1–2 tsp Dijon mustard
lemon juice
salt, pepper

Roasted almonds with smoked salt Serves 2

Pre-heat the oven to 390 °F (200 °C). Mix the salt and oil together, and then mix in the almonds. Spread them over an oven tray covered in baking parchment and roast them in the pre-heated oven for 20 minutes, turning several times until they are golden brown.

Leave the nuts to cool and then store them in a jar.

Serve with fresh flatbreads.

2 tbsp **SMOKED SALT**
2 tbsp oil
2½ cups (250 g) almonds

Oriental lamb casserole Serves 6–8

3¼ lb (1.5 kg) deboned lamb shoulder
2 onions
2 garlic cloves
3 tbsp olive oil
2 tsp each of CUMIN, CORIANDER SEEDS, GROUND GINGER, and GROUND CINNAMON
4 small zucchini
2 red bell peppers
whole mint and parsley leaves to garnish

Cut the lamb shoulder into bite-size pieces. Peel and finely slice the onions and garlic.

Heat the olive oil in a heavy-bottomed casserole dish and add the onions, garlic, and spices. When the onions turn translucent, add the meat.

Pour in enough water to just cover the meat. Bring the water to the boil, then turn down the heat, cover the pot, and leave to simmer gently for 90 minutes.

Meanwhile, wash the zucchini and cut them diagonally into thick slices. Wash, halve and de-seed the peppers, and cut them into thick strips.

Season the cooking liquid with salt and pepper. Add the zucchini and peppers and mix with the meat. Simmer uncovered for another 30 minutes, until the zucchini and pepper pieces are cooked, but still firm to the bite.

Serve scattered with the parsley and mint leaves.

Spinach fritters with yogurt Serves 2

scant ⅓ cup (100 g) frozen spinach (whole leaves)
generous 1 cup (200 g) quinoa
3½ oz cups (100 g) stale bread or breadcrumbs
scant 1 cup (100 g) Pecorino or another hard cheese
2 garlic cloves
3 eggs (medium)
1 tsp TURMERIC
1 tsp CUMIN
2 tbsp oil
natural Greek yogurt to serve
salt, pepper

Thaw and drain the spinach. Press out the remaining water with a kitchen towel, to ensure that the fritters do not become soggy. Rinse the quinoa under warm running water, then add it to 1 pint (½ liter) of salted water and bring to the boil. Leave to simmer over medium heat for approx. 15 minutes, until the quinoa has absorbed the water. Leave to cool and stand.

Meanwhile, crumble the bread. Grate the cheese, and peel and finely chop the garlic. Mix everything together thoroughly with the quinoa, spinach, and eggs. The mixture should hold together well. Season with turmeric, cumin, salt, and pepper.

Using your hands, shape the mixture into 8 fritters. Heat the oil in a large pan over medium heat, and then fry the fritters for 4 minutes. Turn them over and fry for another 2 to 3 minutes. Serve warm with natural yogurt and salad.

This dish goes well with Moroccan chickpea salad (see page 140).

Spotlight on Paprika

The types of paprika produced today are all made from peppers of the *Capsicum annuum* genus. Today the Capiscum family, which is classed as nightshade plants, includes countless species and varieties, which sometimes vary considerably in appearance and color, from fiery-hot chili peppers to sweet bell peppers with thick flesh.

Peppers are thought to have originated in northern Brazil and Colombia. Grave finds prove that peppers were grown and cultivated in Central and South America as early as several millennia BC. Christopher Columbus was responsible for bringing the plant and knowledge about it to Europe.

Peppers were grown for the first time in Spain from the seeds that had been brought back by Columbus. The vegetable, which became known as the Spanish pepper, soon spread over the warm areas of southern Europe. This name is probably a reference to the fact that Christopher Columbus had originally sailed westward in the hope of finding a sea route to India, which would have broken the Arab and Venetian monopoly on pepper.

The pepper plant is ideally suited to widespread cultivation in fields. The most common method of growing it is to cultivate the seedlings in greenhouses before replanting them outdoors once they are strong enough. The plant, which loves warmth, needs nutrient-rich, light soil and constant irrigation. Peppers have been grown in Hungary for centuries, and that country produces considerable quantities of spicy and sweet peppers to this day. Hungarian paprika, which is made from peppers, is classified in grades that have been adopted by most of the other Eastern European lands that produce it, including Serbia, Bulgaria, and Romania. (Other key pepper-growing countries such as Spain, Portugal, and South Africa have not adopted this system of classification.)

The pepper's distinctive piquancy is caused by the alkaloid capsaicin. For a long time, this piquancy was measured in Scoville units. In 1912 the American pharmacologist Wilbur L. Scoville developed a hotness scale that was named after him. Large sweet peppers score between 0 and 10 on the Scoville scale, while extremely hot pepper varieties such as habaneros reach up to 500,000 Scoville units. The measuring method is an organoleptic process, and is not precisely quantifiable due to individual perceptions of heat. Nowadays a system of measuring piquancy through high-performance liquid chromatography (HPLC) tends to be used instead.

Peppers are mainly grown for spice production. Paprika is the most-used spice in the world after pepper.

The quality of paprika can differ greatly. It is worth keeping a lookout for organic produce from smallholders. Mass-produced spices often rely on dehydrating the peppers quickly using large conveyor driers, which often gives the powder a straw-like taste. By contrast, traditionally cultivated peppers that are carefully separated into strings and dried slowly in the sunshine result in the much-prized, full-bodied paprika flavor.

Delicate—mild and fruity
Exquisite delicate—slightly piquant, delicately sweet
Rose—very aromatic and piquant
Hot—yellowish brown and very piquant

Spotlight on Cinnamon: "Brown Gold"

Cinnamon is probably one of the oldest spices in the world, as it appears to have enjoyed massive popularity in Asia as early as 3000 BC. Vasco da Gama brought cinnamon to Europe on his return from India in 1502. It was not long before the spice made its triumphant way from European port cities to Western kitchens. Even today, cinnamon is sometimes described as "brown gold," a reference to the high value placed upon it during this period. For most people it was simply unaffordable. Cinnamon is obtained from the bark of the cinnamon tree, which belongs to the laurel family. A distinction is made between Ceylon cinnamon and Cassia (or Chinese) cinnamon. Strictly speaking, the Cassia variety cannot be considered "genuine" cinnamon. Ceylon cinnamon is fully deserving of its name, as Vasco da Gama transported it from the island of Ceylon, today Sri Lanka, to Portugal in the course of one of his voyages. Yet real cinnamon sets itself above the other variety not only because of its history, but also due to its appearance and fine flavor.

It is relatively easy to distinguish Cassia and Ceylon cinnamon from one another. To make Cassia cinnamon, a layer of the tree bark is simply removed. It curls up when it is dried. For Ceylon cinnamon, however, as many thin strips of bark as possible are interlaid and rolled up to form a multi-layered cinnamon stick. Ceylon cinnamon is also lighter in color.

Cinnamon is commonly used in a lot of baked goods that are popular at Christmas, and in herbal teas in winter. In Sri Lanka, however, it is used almost as often as salt in everyday cooking. Along with the distinctive flavor that it imparts to classic Christmas recipes and many other dishes and drinks, cinnamon also has a healing effect: those who suffer from type 2 diabetes are advised to take cinnamon as a herbal remedy alongside therapy, in order to lower their blood sugar levels and blood pressure.

Buckwheat risotto with beet and scamorza   Serves 4

Peel and finely chop the shallots. Melt the butter in a pan and sweat the shallots. Rinse the buckwheat and fry with the shallots for 2 to 3 minutes.

Meanwhile, peel and grate the beets (wearing disposable gloves will prevent the dye from transferring onto your hands).

Add the wine to the shallots and buckwheat and add the stock gradually, stirring constantly. As soon as the liquid has been absorbed, add a little more stock. After 10 minutes, stir in the beet.

After 20 to 25 minutes the buckwheat should be cooked. Season with salt, pepper, and the smoked paprika. Grate the cheese and stir it into the risotto. Divide the risotto between 4 plates and serve.

2 shallots
2 tbsp butter
generous 2 cups (400 g) buckwheat
2 fresh beets
⅔ cups (150 ml) white wine
approx. 1 quart (1 liter) hot chicken stock
salt, pepper
¼ tsp **SMOKED PAPRIKA**
5½ oz (150 g) scamorza (about 9 slices)

Chestnut soup with hazelnuts   Serves 4

Peel and dice the shallot and carrot. Chop the chestnuts finely. Heat 1 tablespoon of oil in a pot and fry the shallot gently, before adding the carrot and continuing to fry briefly. Add the white wine, and then the stock and cinnamon, and leave everything to simmer for 10 to 15 minutes.

While the mixture is simmering, toast the hazelnuts in a dry pan until they give off a pleasant aroma. Leave to cool briefly and then chop them roughly.

Add the chestnuts and cream to the soup 3 minutes before the end of the cooking time.

Remove the cinnamon stick from the soup. Blend the soup until it is smooth, and season to taste with salt and pepper. Ladle the soup into 4 bowls and garnish with hazelnuts.

A slice of fruit loaf or sourdough bread would make a good accompaniment to this soup.

1 shallot
1 carrot
3 cups (400 g) roasted chestnuts
2 tbsp oil
3½ tbsp (50 ml) white wine
3½ cups (800 ml) vegetable stock
1 **CINNAMON STICK**
6 tbsp cream
¾ cup (100 g) hazelnuts
salt, pepper

Couscous salad with mushrooms Serves 4

1¼ cups (250 g) couscous
3 tbsp olive oil
salt
11 oz (300 g) mixed mushrooms
½ tsp GROUND CINNAMON
pepper
1 garlic clove
generous ¾ cup yogurt
2 tbsp tahini (sesame paste)
juice of 1 lemon
½ tsp CUMIN
½ bunch of parsley
½ cup (100 g) dried figs
¾ cup (75 g) almonds

Mix the couscous with 1 tablespoon of oil and 1 teaspoon of salt and pour over boiling water until it is just covered. Place a lid or a plate over the bowl and leave to stand for 10 to 15 minutes. Once the time is up, fluff up the couscous with a fork.

Clean and chop the mushrooms. Heat 2 tablespoons of olive oil in a pan and sear the mushrooms until they are golden brown all over. Season with cinnamon and pepper and set to one side.

To make the dressing, peel and crush the garlic clove, and mix it with the yogurt, tahini, lemon juice and cumin. Season with salt.

Chop the parsley finely and dice the figs. Toast the almonds in a dry pan and then chop roughly. Mix the parsley, figs, and almonds into the couscous. Add the mushrooms and drizzle over the dressing.

Beet salad with goat's milk cheese Serves 4

1¾ lb (800 g) fresh beets
2 tbsp dark wild honey
8 coffee beans
7 tbsp (100 ml) olive oil
3½ tbsp (50 ml) cherry vinegar
2 lamb's lettuces
½ cup (60 g) walnuts
4 small round goat's milk cheeses
LONG PEPPER
4 smoked trout fillets

Pre-heat the oven to 350 °F (180 °C). Peel the beets and cut them into pieces (wearing disposable gloves will prevent the natural dye transferring to your hands). Mix the honey, coffee beans, oil, and vinegar with the beets and spread the mixture over a baking tray. Bake the beets for 25 to 30 minutes.

In the meantime, wash and toss the lamb's lettuce.

When the beets are cooked and slightly caramelized, take them out of the oven and remove the coffee beans.

Toast the walnuts in a dry pan. Season the goat's milk cheeses with freshly ground long pepper and place the cheeses and some beet on a bed of lamb's lettuce on each plate. Scatter the nuts over the salad and serve with the trout.

Mango and turmeric ice cream   Serves 4

Heat two-thirds of the coconut milk gently in a pot together with the sugar until the coconut oil melts. Mix the rest of the coconut milk with the arrowroot and stir into the warm coconut milk. Add the turmeric and a pinch of salt. Bring to the boil, stirring constantly, so that the starch begins to bind. Leave the mixture to cool.

Purée the mango and add it to the coconut milk along with the Greek yogurt. Leave it to freeze in the ice cream maker for approximately 25 minutes, before placing in the freezer to deep freeze for at least 1 hour. Take the ice cream out of the freezer at least 30 minutes before serving. This ice cream will go very well with an exotic fruit salad.

1 can of coconut milk (400 ml)
generous ¾ cup (160 g) sugar
1 tbsp arrowroot
1 tsp **TURMERIC**
1 ripe mango
scant 1½ cups (400 g) Greek yogurt
salt

Tonka ice cream with hazelnut brittle   Serves 4

To make the ice cream, slice the vanilla pod in half lengthways and scrape out the seeds. Warm the milk, tonka beans, scraped-out vanilla pod and pulp in a pot, then cover and leave to stand for 30 minutes.

Using a handheld whisk, beat the egg yolks and sugar until fluffy. Add the warm tonka milk mixture in a thin stream, stirring constantly. Pour the mixture back into the pot and warm through over medium heat, continuing to stir, until the creamy mixture has reached 170 to 174 °F (77 to 79 °C)—a kitchen thermometer is best for taking the temperature. Under no circumstances should it come to the boil.

Strain the mixture through a sieve. Add the cream, cover, and leave to stand in a cold place for 2 to 3 hours or overnight. Transfer the ice cream mixture to an ice cream maker. Once the ice cream is ready, put it in a suitable container and leave to deep freeze in the freezer.

To make the hazelnut brittle, heat 4 tablespoons of water, the sugar, and the butter in a pan. When the mixture turns light brown, add the hazelnuts. Turn down the heat and carry on stirring.

When the caramel is golden brown, remove the pan from the heat. Spread the caramel onto baking parchment. Sprinkle with fleur de sel, leave it to cool, and then break it into pieces.

Remove the ice cream from the freezer 30 minutes before serving. Decorate with the hazelnut brittle.

For the ice cream
1 vanilla pod
1⅔ cups (400 ml) milk
2 **TONKA BEANS**
5 egg yolks
7 tbsp (100 g) sugar
¾ cup (200 g) whipping cream

For the hazelnut brittle
7 tbsp (100 g) sugar
3½ tbsp butter
¾ cup (100 g) chopped hazelnuts
½ tsp fleur de sel

Warning: *Because of high coumarin levels, it is advised to use tonka beans sparingly (see p. 27).*

Poppy seed whirls Makes 20

For the dough
Grated zest of ½ lemon
4 cups (530 g) flour
7 tbsp (100 g) sugar
1½ tsp (20 g) fresh yeast
3 eggs
½ cup (120 ml) lukewarm water
⅔ cup (150 g) cubed butter, at room
   temperature
salt

For the filling
1¼ cups (300 ml) milk
1½ cups (200 g) ground poppy seeds
7 tbsp (100 g) sugar
⅓ cup (80 g) butter
1 tsp GROUND CINNAMON

To make the dough, put the lemon zest, flour, sugar, and a pinch of salt in a bowl. Crumble the yeast and add to the flour mixture with the eggs and the water. Knead to form a smooth dough using the dough hook of a mixer.

Add the cubes of butter and knead for another 10 minutes, using the middle setting. Cover the dough and leave in a warm place to prove for about 1 hour.

To make the filling, put the milk in a pan, add the poppy seeds, and bring the mixture to the boil. Leave to simmer for approximately 30 minutes, until it is creamy. Stir in the sugar, butter, and cinnamon, and leave to cool.

Divide the dough into two portions and roll each of these out to form a rectangle. Spread each rectangle with half of the poppy seed filling, and then roll the rectangles up tightly.

Cut the rolls into slices approximately 1½ inches (4 cm) wide and place them on a baking tray covered in baking parchment. Leave to prove for another hour.

Heat the oven to 390 °F (200 °C) and bake the rolls for about 15 to 20 minutes on the middle tray.

Chocolate beet cake Serves 4

generous ¾ cup (200 g) butter
½ cup (150 g) honey
1 cup (200 g) dark chocolate
   (minimum 75% cocoa content), grated
4 tbsp freshly brewed espresso
5 eggs
1 cup (250 g) beet purée
1 cup (150 g) spelt flour
2 tsp baking powder
3 tbsp cocoa powder
pinch of salt
1 tsp GROUND CINNAMON

Pre-heat the oven to 350 °F (175 °C). Warm the butter in a pot over low heat. Add the honey and chocolate. Stir together until the chocolate is completely melted. Add the hot espresso and remove the pot from the stove.

Separate the eggs. Whisk the egg yolks and stir them swiftly and evenly into the slightly cooled chocolate mixture.

Fold in the beet purée. Beat the egg whites until they form stiff peaks, and fold them into the chocolate mixture in turn.

Sieve the flour, baking powder, and cocoa powder into a bowl, add the salt and cinnamon, and mix together. Fold into the chocolate mixture.

Grease an 8-inch (20-cm) cake tin. Pour in the batter and bake in the hot oven for 25 to 30 minutes. Take the cake out of the oven and leave to cool for 15 minutes before turning it out of the tin.

Fragrant and Delicate:

Floral Spices

Floral spices offer notes on the nose and palate that are particularly popular amongst connoisseurs. Their flavor is never simple, and always makes for a sensory feast, as they often have a creamy or lemony edge that can really make the different in desserts, sauces, and drinks. The scent of vanilla at once calms and promotes inner balance. Lemongrass and orange blossom, on the other hand, not only invigorate the mind, but also enliven any dish in which they are used. Elderberries and rose petals enrich delicate flavors. Precious saffron is remarkable on several levels: not only does it make wonderfully smooth sauces, but it also provides that saturated shade of yellow that stimulates the appetite. Its taste is subtle yet unforgettable. Floral spices may be delicate, but they punch well above their weight in terms of taste.

Lavender

Origins and cultivation

True or narrow-leaf lavender belongs to the mint family and is a shrub that can grow up to about 3 feet (1 meter) high. It originated from the coastal areas of the Mediterranean, where it thrives on sunny, rocky slopes. Lavender can be found from southern France to Greece, and is also grown in plantations. In Provence the blooming lavender fields are a veritable tourist attraction, but in most cases these fields of purple are not true lavender but instead a hybrid variety, lavandin, which is primarily grown by the pharmaceutical industry to produce essential oils and used as a base for herbal extracts. True lavender can now be bought from almost any garden center, and the plant will love any sunny patch in your garden at home.

History

Benedictine monks introduced true lavender to areas north of the Alps in the 17th century. As true lavender is a hardy perennial that occurs at up to 6,000 feet (1,800 meters), the plant soon acclimatized to temperate regions all over the world.

Use

In the kitchen, flowers with young shoots make a popular and sophisticated addition to fish dishes, stews, and even roast lamb. True lavender is also important in medicine. The dried flowers have been credited as a remedy for gall bladder problems. Lavender products have also been successful in treating nervous disorders and migraines. The essential oil produced by steam distillation is popular in pharmacies as a valuable natural base for many medicinal preparations. As the nectar within the flowers has a high sugar content, beekeepers prize the flowers when they are in bloom, and lavender honey is a healthy delicacy.

Rose petals

Origins and history

The type of rose that is usually encountered today is the *Rosa canina*, generally known as the dog rose. The scientific name is taken from the Latin word for a dog. It is thought that in centuries gone by the rose root was commonly used as a remedy against rabies—hence the rose's botanical name. Other parent species include the *Rosa centifolia* and the *Rosa gallica*, and there are myriad other subspecies and varieties. The *Rosa centifolia* has bright red to pale red petals, while those of the *Rosa gallica* tend to be dark red. Rose petals were used in cooking as early as the 9th century. In Persia, in particular, the buds and petals were considered a premium, precious spice, and using them was the sole preserve of the highest echelons of society. In some Balkan countries rose oil is largely made from the *Rosa damascena*. The production process is extremely labor-intensive: almost 4 tons of petals are needed to make 1 quart (1 liter) of rose oil.

Use

The fragrance of dried rose petals gives sweets, cakes, and desserts a very appealing taste. Rose petals are used in India, North Africa, and the Middle East to flavor certain dairy products. They are also added to meat dishes to refine the taste, including the braised lamb specialties served all over Morocco and Tunisia. Rose petals are fantastic for flavoring sugar. Simply mix 7 tablespoons of sugar with 1⅓ oz (10 g) of rose petals and leave to stand for a few days. The delicate floral rose flavor will infuse the sugar.

Saffron

Origins and cultivation

Saffron has been a highly popular spice for centuries. Not for nothing has it been dubbed "the spice of kings." Its plant, a type of crocus (*Crocus sativus*) that belongs to the iris family, originally came from the Aegean Islands and Crete. Today it is mainly cultivated in Spain, Greece, and Iran.

Interesting facts

The spice known as saffron consists of the three reddish-brown stigmas found at the end of the flower's pistil. Harvesting them is extremely laborious: about 200,000 blooming flowers are needed to make 2 pounds (1 kg) of saffron, and the stigmas are plucked from each of them by hand. It is no surprise, then, that saffron has always been the most expensive spice of all, and its sheer value has meant that fraudsters have always attempted to sell bogus versions. In the Middle Ages, faking saffron incurred draconian punishments. Records show, for example, that in 1443 Jobst Findeker from Nuremberg was burned alive along with his fake saffron. However, that terrible sentence clearly did not act as much of a deterrent. In 1456 more Nuremberg saffron merchants were burned along with their counterfeit wares. Similar sentences were handed down in Switzerland. Even today, bogus spices are sold on a massive scale, often containing turmeric. In countries such as Morocco, Tunisia, and Turkey, the dried disk flowers of the fake saffron plant are even sold at "bargain" prices to unsuspecting tourists as "safflower."

Use

The water-soluble pigment in saffron is called crocetin, and it is so intense that three small stigmas are enough to dye three quarts (3 liters) of water a golden hue. Saffron is used in cooking, albeit in very small quantities, not only for its coloring but also for its tangy and slightly bitter flavor. Saffron should not be cooked with food for long if it is to preserve its taste. One handy tip is to soak the saffron stigmas in lukewarm water for a few minutes, and then to add only the brightly colored water to your cooking. Saffron is used in a range of dishes, including paellas, the southern French soup bouillabaisse, and Italian risottos. It also works particularly well in creamy sauces to accompany fish and seafood. A little saffron stirred into a cake mixture or pasta dough also has a pleasing effect, not least because of its golden color.

Lemongrass

Cultivation

Lemongrass belongs to the grass family and is mainly cultivated on large plantations in Southeast Asia. It is as popular and widespread there as chives and parsley are in the West. The reed-like stalks of these grass varieties can reach heights of up to 6½ feet (2 meters).

Use

Lemongrass is primarily found in Asian cuisine, and it tends to be used fresh. It is possible to buy dried lemongrass, which is sold under the name of sereh. However, this dried version is not particularly popular as it loses its appealing lemony flavor during the dehydration process. You should beat the lemongrass stalks hard before actually using them, in order to release the essential oils. Lemongrass is also used in many blends of tea for its thirst-quenching properties. Citral, which is extracted from the essential oil, is used on an industrial scale as a base substance and fragrance in soaps, shampoos, and cosmetics.

Vanilla

Origins and history

True vanilla, which belongs to the orchid family, originally comes from Central America. The genus encompasses several species. The scientific name for the variety that is popular as a spice is *Vanilla planifolia*. Vanilla was prized by the Aztecs, who used it to flavor their bitter cocoa drink. It reached Europe relatively late. When Mexico became independent in 1810 and, for a short time, exporting it was no longer subject to draconian punishments, cuttings of the wild vanilla plant were grown in botanical gardens in France and Belgium. Yet it was the Dutch who, in 1819, pilfered vanilla sprouts from Mexico (where exporting had since become strictly prohibited once again) and succeeded in cultivating it in Java and on Bourbon Island, now Réunion. But there was a major problem: the flowers did not bear fruit, and simply fell off the plant without being pollinated. The reason for this was simple: the insects that were vital to the pollination of vanilla were endemic to Central America, and did not exist in the Indian Ocean. In 1837 the German horticulturist Joseph Henri François Neumann finally succeeded in growing a fruit on a vanilla plant through artificial pollination in the botanical gardens in Paris. A year later, the same feat was achieved by a Belgian expert at the botanical gardens in Liège.

Cultivation

To this day, the need for artificial pollination and the costs associated with this process mean that vanilla pods are relatively expensive. Vanilla is now grown on plantations. A climbing plant, it winds up round stakes up to 10 feet (3 meters) high. A type of orchid, it produces inconspicuous little white flowers. When the flowers open, the petals are artificially pollinated using very fine brushes. The elongated green pods that form later are picked by hand and have to undergo an elaborate fermentation process. Stores then sell the now brown-black vanilla pods, which contain vanilla pulp. Today, the main growing areas are Madagascar, which covers 80 percent of the global demand, as well as Indonesia, Réunion, Tahiti, Mexico, and various Caribbean islands.

Use

Sugar can be flavored with vanilla by keeping a vanilla pod in an airtight sugar box. You can make the base for vanilla sauce by bringing cream or milk to the boil with vanilla. Vanilla can also be used to flavor desserts such as crème brûlée and panna cotta.

Oranges and orange blossom

Origins and history

Oranges, a cross between tangerines and pomelos, are thought to originate from China or Southeast Asia. When Portuguese sailors discovered the sea route to India in the 15th century, they brought oranges back with them to Europe. Since then they have become the most grown citrus fruit in the world, and are cultivated on a massive scale, reaching far beyond the Mediterranean. Indeed, the biggest orange producers are Brazil and the USA.

Use

Orange zest is widely used in desserts, cakes, and savory dishes owing to its essential oils. By contrast, orange blossom is—quite unjustly—a relatively unknown ingredient, used by only a handful of connoisseurs. For quite some time, it has been most known largely for its calming and soporific effect in tea blends. Yet both fresh and dried orange blossoms offer a wealth of possibilities in the kitchen. The subtly floral, honey-like, somewhat herbal flavor—which is only slightly redolent of oranges—, develops wonderfully in desserts, cakes, and marmalades. And both Indian and oriental dishes attest to the fact that the herbal sweetness of orange blossom works very well in lamb dishes, ragouts, sauces, and salads, too.

English scones with saffron Makes 12

4⅔ cups (700 g) flour
2 tsp baking powder
1 tsp bicarbonate of soda
2⅓ cups (75 g) sugar
1 cup + 2 tbsp (250 g) ice-cold butter, cubed
½ tsp SAFFRON THREADS
generous 1½ cups (375 ml) buttermilk
1 tsp salt
1 packet of candied orange peel

Pre-heat the oven to 350 °F (175 °C) and cover a baking tray with baking parchment. Mix the flour, baking powder, bicarbonate of soda, and salt thoroughly together in a large bowl. Stir in the sugar. Add the cubes of butter and work them into the flour mixture using a dough scraper or your fingertips. You should end up with a crumbly texture.

Crush the saffron in a mortar with a pinch of sugar, pour over 1 tablespoon of boiling water, and mix with the buttermilk. Stir this into the flour mixture, but only until the flour has been folded in. You should still be able to see bits of butter. Finally, fold the orange peel carefully into the dough.

Turn the dough out of the bowl and onto a lightly floured surface. Carefully roll it out so that it is 2 inches (5 cm) thick. Cut it into 12 triangular pieces. Place the scones on the baking tray, leaving space between them.

Bake the scones for about 25 to 30 minutes in the lower third of the oven, until they are slightly browned. Remove them from the tray and place on a cooling rack. Serve gently warmed, perhaps with orange marmalade.

Orange blossom fougasse Serves 4

For the orange blossom syrup
7 tbsp water
7 tbsp (100 g) sugar
5 g dried ORANGE BLOSSOMS

For the dough
3½ tbsp (50 ml) lukewarm milk
½ tsp (8 g) fresh yeast
1¾ cups (250 g) flour
4 tbsp (50 g) olive oil
7 tbsp (100 g) orange blossom syrup
1 tbsp butter

Tip

If you cannot obtain orange blossoms, mix 1 tablespoon of orange blossom water with 3½ tablespoons (50 g) sugar and 3½ tablespoons (50 ml) cold water, and then stir this into the dough. You could serve any leftover syrup as a cold drink.

To make the orange blossom syrup, warm the water and sugar in a pot until the sugar has dissolved. Add the orange blossoms and bring to the boil, then turn down the heat and leave to simmer for 5 minutes.

Remove the syrup from the heat and leave to stand for 2 hours. Strain it through a sieve and pour into a clean glass.

To make the dough, mix the lukewarm milk with the yeast. Sieve the flour onto a clean surface and form a well in the middle. Pour the milk mixture, olive oil, and orange blossom syrup into the well and mix in, drawing flour little by little from the edge of the well. Leave this starter dough in a warm place for 30 minutes to prove.

Add the butter and knead the dough for about 10 minutes until it is stretchy. Leave in a warm place for 2 hours to prove.

Place the dough on a floured surface, press it flat with your fingertips, and then roll it out to form an oval shape. Cut it in half lengthways. Make three more short cuts to the right and left of the middle, at a 45-degree angle. Leave to prove for another 30 minutes. Heat the oven to 430 °F (220 °C) and bake the fougasse for 20 minutes.

Vanilla and tomato jam   Makes 2 jars, each 1 lb (450 ml)

2¼ lb (1 kg) green tomatoes
1 lemon
2 VANILLA PODS
1½ cups (300 g) preserving sugar

Cut the tomatoes into quarters. Zest the lemon, then cut it in half and press out the juice. Mix the tomatoes and lemon juice and zest with the vanilla pods and the preserving sugar, and leave to stand overnight.

Next day, bring the mixture gradually to the boil and leave to simmer for about 40 minutes. Keep stirring it gently the whole time. Wash out the jam jars with boiling water. Pour the jam into them. You can take the vanilla pods out beforehand if you wish, or simply put them into the jars along with the jam.

This jam goes well with cheese.

Fried zucchini flowers with lavender Serves 4

Wash the zucchini flowers carefully and pat them dry, then cut out the pistils and stamens. Mix the lemon zest with the fresh goat's milk cheese and fill the flowers with the mixture.

Mix the flour with ½ teaspoon salt, pepper, and the lavender blossoms. Separate the egg. Mix the yolk and wine into the flour mixture using a whisk. Place the egg white in a cool place. Leave the dough to stand for 30 minutes.

Beat the egg white so that it forms stiff peaks, then fold it into the dough.

Heat the oil in a pot or deep fryer. Push the flowers through the dough one after another and deep fry them in the oil in batches. When they are golden brown, remove them from the oil, leave to dry off on kitchen paper, season with salt, and serve warm.

These zucchini flowers make an ideal starter, served with a green salad.

generous 1 lb (500 g) zucchini flowers
grated zest of 1 lemon
generous 1 cup (250 g) fresh goat's milk cheese
generous 1 cup (150 g) flour
1 tbsp **LAVENDER BLOSSOMS**
1 egg (large)
⅔ cup (150 ml) white wine
1 quart (1 liter) oil for deep frying
salt, pepper

Cucumber yogurt with rose petals Serves 4

Peel and grate the cucumber. Wrap the grated cucumber in a tea towel and press out the excess moisture.

Peel the garlic cloves and chop finely together with the mint leaves. Mix into the yogurt and add salt to taste. Garnish with rose petals.

1 cucumber
2 garlic cloves
2 sprigs of fresh mint
1¾ cups (500 g) Greek yogurt
2 tsp dried **ROSE PETALS**
½ tsp salt

White asparagus tart with flower blossoms Serves 4

For the pastry
1¾ cups (250 g) flour
⅔ cup (150 g) butter
1½ tsp fleur de sel
baking beans

For the filling
14 oz (400 g) white asparagus
generous ¾ cup (200 g) crème fraîche
1 egg
grated zest of ½ lemon
1 tbsp **DRIED EDIBLE FLOWERS**
   (e.g. cornflower, lavender, orange, thyme,
   violet blossoms)
salt, pepper

To make the pastry, mix the flour, butter, and salt to a crumbly consistency with your hands. Add 2 tablespoons of ice-cold water and knead until you can form a ball. Wrap the pastry in plastic wrap and place in the refrigerator for about 1 hour.

Pre-heat the oven to 355 °F (180 °C). Roll the pastry out onto a lightly floured surface, and then place it in a tart tin, pressing the sides firmly.

Place a circle of baking parchment on top of the pastry and cover it with baking beans. Bake in the oven for 15 minutes, then take out and remove the baking beans and baking parchment.

Meanwhile, to make the filling, peel the asparagus, cut off the woody ends, and blanch the spears in boiling water. Drain and leave to dry.

Mix the crème fraîche and egg with the lemon zest and dried flowers, then season with salt and pepper. Spoon the mixture into the tart case and place the asparagus on top. Bake in the oven for 25 minutes.

A green salad with berry vinegar vinaigrette would make a good accompaniment to this tart.

Raspberry and rose crumble Serves 4

generous 1 lb (500 g) raspberries
   (frozen or fresh)
1 tbsp **ROSE PETALS**
4½ tbsp (60 g) cane sugar
⅔ cup (100 g) flour
2 tbsp shredded coconut
7 tbsp soft butter + extra for greasing the tin
2 tbsp pistachios, chopped
pinch of salt

Wash the fresh raspberries or thaw the frozen raspberries. Pre-heat the oven to 390 °F (200 °C). Crush the rose petals and sugar finely in a mortar. Using your fingers, work the rose sugar, flour, shredded coconut, salt, and butter to a crumbly consistency.

Grease a baking dish and spread the raspberries over the bottom of it. Scatter over the crumble mixture and bake in the oven for approx. 20 minutes. Sprinkle with the chopped pistachios. This goes well with tonka ice cream (see page 43).

Oven-baked seabream with lemongrass and zucchini Serves 4

3 small, prepared gilthead seabream,
  each approx. 11 oz (300 g)
2 garlic cloves
8 stalks of **LEMONGRASS**
4 zucchini
2 unwaxed lemons
2 tbsp olive oil
fleur de sel, pepper

Pre-heat the oven to 390 °F (200 °C). Rinse the fish under running water. Pat them dry with kitchen towel and place them on three separate pieces of baking parchment.

Peel and chop the garlic cloves. Beat the thick ends of the lemongrass stalks flat and cut the stalks into pieces. Cut the zucchini into thin strips lengthways. Slice the lemons, and then cut each slice in half.

Stuff the lemongrass, garlic, and lemon slices into the cleaned-out fish. Season the inside and outside of the fish with salt and pepper.

Wrap the seabream in the zucchini strips and drizzle with olive oil. Wrap the backing parchment round the fish, crinkle the sides, and twist at the top so that the parcel looks like a sweet, and then secure the parcel with butcher's string. Place the parcels on a baking tray and bake in the oven for approx. 20 minutes.

Vanilla risotto Serves 4

Peel the shallot and dice it finely. Cut the vanilla pod in half lengthways and scrape out the pulp using the back of a knife.

Heat the olive oil in a pot and sauté the shallot until it is translucent, then add the rice and fry briefly.

Add the white wine, and then gradually pour in the hot vegetable stock, stirring constantly. Add the vanilla pod and pulp. Cook the rice for approx. 20 minutes, stirring all the while, until it is firm to the bite.

Just before the end of the cooking time, fold the grated Parmesan into the risotto. Remove the vanilla pod and season the risotto to taste with salt and pepper.

Divide the risotto between 4 plates.

1 shallot
1 **VANILLA POD**
2 tbsp olive oil
1½ cups (300 g) Arborio rice
7 tbsp white wine
3⅓ cups vegetable stock
¾ cup (75 g) Parmesan, finely grated
salt, pepper

Tip

This risotto makes a good accompaniment to pike-perch pan-fried with vanilla. Cut 1¼ lb (600 g) pike-perch fillets into 4 pieces each, season with salt and pepper, and fry in 2 tablespoons of olive oil together with the vanilla pod from the risotto for approx. 4 minutes.

Veal tenderloin with lavender glaze and blackberries Serves 4

Chop the green asparagus, celery, and scallions roughly. Wash the blackberries carefully. Stir the lavender honey, lavender blossoms, and white wine together to make a marinade.

Heat 1 tablespoon of butter in an ovenproof pan and fry the vegetables for 5 to 6 minutes. Season with salt and pepper. Remove the vegetables from the pan and keep warm.

Add the remaining butter to the pan. Rub the veal tenderloin with salt and sear on all sides. Pour over the marinade and cook in the oven for approx. 15 minutes, then cover the pan with aluminum foil and leave to stand for 5 to 6 minutes.

Add the blackberries and balsamic vinegar to the pan and warm through. Slice the veal tenderloin and serve with the vegetables and blackberries.

14 oz (400 g) green asparagus
2 sticks of celery
2 scallions
2½ cups (250 g) blackberries
3 tbsp lavender honey
1 tbsp **LAVENDER BLOSSOMS**
7 tbsp white wine
2 tbsp butter
generous 1 lb (500 g) veal tenderloin
1 tbsp balsamic vinegar
salt, pepper

Tomato soup with lemongrass Serves 4

1 onion
⅓-inch (1-cm) piece of fresh ginger
2 tbsp olive oil
1¾ lb (750 g) tomatoes
2½ cups (600 ml) vegetable stock
2 stalks of **LEMONGRASS**
2 kaffir lime leaves (if available)
Espelette pepper
Thai basil (or normal basil)
salt

Peel and dice the onion and ginger, then sauté them in olive oil until they are transparent.

Wash the tomatoes, remove the cores, and chop roughly. Add to the onion and pour over the vegetable stock.

Beat the lemongrass flatter with a rolling pin and add it to the soup together with the kaffir lime leaves. After it has been simmering for 30 minutes, remove the lime leaves and lemongrass from the soup.

Purée the soup using a stick blender. Season with salt and Espelette pepper. Garnish with Thai basil.

Melon gazpacho with rose petals Serves 4

3¼ lb (1.5 kg) cantaloupe melon
2 shallots
1¼ lb (600 g) tomatoes
juice of 1 lemon
2 tbsp brown sugar
1 tbsp **ROSE PETALS** or 2 tbsp rosewater
3 tbsp olive oil
2 sprigs of fresh lemon verbena to decorate
salt, pepper

Halve the melons, scoop out the seeds, and chop the flesh roughly. Peel the shallots and cut them into quarters. Wash the tomatoes, cut them into wedges, and remove the cores.

Purée the melon, shallots, and tomatoes with the rest of the ingredients until the gazpacho is smooth. Season to taste with salt and pepper. Chill, and garnish with the lemon verbena.

Serve with freshly baked French bread.

Warm roasted pepper salad with saffron Serves 4

Brush the peppers with a little olive oil, place them on a baking tray, and grill for 8 minutes on each side. When the skin begins to form black blisters, remove them from the heat. Cover with a damp tea towel and leave to stand for 10 minutes. Skin, halve, and de-seed the peppers and cut them into strips.

Meanwhile, cook the orzo pasta according to the packet instructions until it is firm to the bite. Drain and rinse with cold water. Mix a little olive oil into the orzo so that it does not stick together.

Zest half of the orange peel, then cut the orange in half, and squeeze out the juice. Put the orange juice, zest, olive oil, vinegar, and a little salt in a pan and simmer for 5 minutes.

Crush the saffron threads in a mortar and then leave them to dissolve in 1 tablespoon of the warm marinade. Mix everything together with the pepper strips. Mix the peppers and their marinade with the orzo.

Toast the almonds and chop them roughly. Cube the feta and scatter over the salad together with the almonds.

3 bell peppers (yellow and red)
1 cup (200 g) orzo (Greek short-cut pasta)
4 tbsp olive oil + extra for brushing and for the pasta
1 unwaxed orange
1 tbsp light balsamic vinegar
½ tsp **SAFFRON THREADS**
¾ cup (75 g) almonds
1⅓ cups (200 g) feta cheese
salt

Strawberry salad with roasted asparagus and vanilla vinaigrette Serves 4

Wash and toss the salad leaves. Remove the woody ends off the asparagus spears and cut them into pieces. Wash and hull the strawberries and cut into quarters.

Heat 1 tablespoon of olive oil in a pan and sauté the asparagus for approx. 5 to 7 minutes. Season with salt and pepper and add to the wild-herb salad.

To make the vinaigrette, scrape out the pulp of the vanilla pod and mix with the raspberry vinegar, 2 tablespoons of olive oil, Dijon mustard, and a little salt. Drizzle the vinaigrette over the salad and scatter pieces of ricotta on top.

5 cups (150 g) wild-herb leaves or baby spinach, packed
1 bundle of green asparagus
2½ cups (250 g) strawberries
3 tbsp olive oil
½ **VANILLA POD**
1 tbsp raspberry vinegar
½ tsp Dijon mustard
1 cup (250 g) ricotta

Tip

This salad goes well with fresh rosemary focaccia.

Orange blossom tart Makes 1 tart

For the pastry
1¾ cups (250 g) flour
⅓ cup (80 g) butter
9 tbsp sugar
pinch of salt
1 egg yolk

For the filling
1 **VANILLA POD**
2 cups (500 ml) milk
1 tbsp **ORANGE BLOSSOM** or 1 tbsp orange
    blossom water
4 egg yolks
7 tbsp sugar
7 tbsp flour
7½ cups (750 g) strawberries

To make the dough, work the flour, butter, sugar, and salt to a breadcrumb consistency with your fingers. Add the egg yolk and continue to knead until you can form a ball with the dough. Wrap it in plastic wrap and leave in the refrigerator for about 1 hour.

Pre-heat the oven to 390 °F (200 °C). Roll the dough out onto a floured surface. Place it in a greased tart tin, press the sides, and tidy the edges. Prick the floor of the flan case several times with a fork. Place the tin on the middle oven shelf and bake for about 20 minutes. Leave to cool completely.

While the tart case is baking, scrape out the vanilla pod. To make the filling, pour the milk into a pot and heat it along with the orange blossom, vanilla pod, and vanilla pulp until it is almost at boiling point.

Beat the egg yolk and sugar in a bowl until they form a creamy mixture. Add the flour and stir until smooth. Slowly add half of the milk to the egg mixture, beating constantly with the egg whisk. Add the rest of the milk and the orange blossom water, if using. Beat once again and then pour the mixture back into the pot. Bring the mixture to the boil and let it thicken for 1 minute, stirring constantly. Remove from the heat and take out the orange blossoms and vanilla pod.

Leave the filling to cool and then spread it over the bottom of the pastry case. Wash and hull the strawberries and cut them into quarters, then arrange in a circle on top of the filling and press them down lightly. Serve chilled.

Vanilla flan Makes 4 small flans

1 **VANILLA POD**
1⅔ cups (400 ml) whole milk
4 eggs
4 ½ tbsp sugar

Cut the vanilla pod in half lengthways and scrape out the pulp. Put the milk, vanilla pulp, and vanilla pod in a pan, bring the mixture to the boil, and then leave it to stand for 10 minutes.

Pre-heat the oven to 300 °F (150 °C). Remove the vanilla pod from the milk. Mix the eggs and sugar. Gradually add the milk to the egg mixture.

Place the small flan tins on a deep-rimmed baking tray and pour the filling into the tins. Fill the baking tray with water until it comes up to ⅓ inch (1 cm) under the edge of the flan tins. Place in the oven and bake for approx. 1 hour. The flans are ready when they feel springy to the touch.

Take the flans out of the oven and leave them to cool. To serve, cut round the edge with a knife to free them from the tins, and turn them out.

Spices with Staying Power:

Balsamic Flavors

Anyone who has ever bitten into a juniper berry, cardamom pod, or a stick of licorice will be familiar with the intense burst of flavor that comes from these woody spices. In terms of taste, they span the full range from medicinal and herbal to heavy and syrupy, while orange and bergamot provide perfumed notes. Fennel and star anise offer ostensibly opposite tastes, such as bitter and sweet, in the very same spice. Balsamic herbs—basil, rosemary, and thyme—harbor a wealth of tastes that, when they are properly cooked or worked into dishes, lend food an enduring flavor that is quite unlike anything else. And in addition to their full-bodied taste, these plants are all-rounders, too, with medicinal properties. Sage, for instance, has been proved to have analgesic effects, and may also ward off premature labor. When used in cooking it is proven to promote digestion, as are juniper berries, cardamom, and fennel. Balsamic spices tend to be capricious yet virtuoso flavor carriers due to their often resinous notes, which in some cases blend into subtly bitter flavors.

Basil

Origins and history

Basil (*Ocimum basilicum*) belongs to the mint family. There is some dispute amongst experts about the origins of this popular herb. Today basil is endemic to tropical regions of Africa and Asia, in particular India, and it is also found in moderate areas round the Mediterranean. Artefacts discovered in the Egyptian pyramids prove that this aromatic and medicinal plant (used as a remedy for digestive disorders and to allay inflammation) was cultivated and frequently used in ancient times. Basil has been well known in Europe since the early Middle Ages. The name "basil" comes from the Greek word *basileus*, which means "king," and in many regions basil is still known as the "king of herbs."

Cultivation

The collective term "basil" now covers many varieties of the basil family, which often differ greatly in size, leaf shape, and flavor. Full-scale basil plantations are confined to subtropical areas.

The foremost exporters of basil are India, Morocco, and southern Spain, where the type of basil that is most suitable for drying is mainly grown. Fresh basil, which is particularly popular, is cultivated in greenhouses and then sold in its pot or in bunches. Basil prefers warm temperatures, and it cannot really grow under 59 °F (15 °C). The plant can be propagated not only by sowing seeds, but also by taking cuttings, which can be placed in a glass of water to form roots. Using this method allows everyone to have an easy and endless supply of basil at home.

Use

Basil is one of the most-used herbs in Italian cuisine, making an appearance in traditional favorites such as fresh basil leaves with tomato and mozzarella. It is normally also the main ingredient in green pesto. In its dried form, used as a rub, basil is also great for seasoning sauces and meat and fish dishes.

Bergamot

Origins and cultivation

Bergamot is a hybrid—a cross between bitter orange and citron. This citrus fruit is cultivated less for its fruits than for its intense fragrance. Bergamot comes from the tip of the "boot" of Italy. The plantations where it is cultivated lie in a relatively narrow coastal strip in Calabria, between Melito di Porto Salvo and Reggio Calabria. These supply the pharmaceutical and perfume industries with bergamot essential oil, which is obtained from the thick and highly aromatic yellow peel of the bergamot fruit. About 550 pounds (250 kg) of fully ripe fruits are needed to make a quart (1 liter) of this essential oil.

Use

As a raw fruit, bergamot is not really edible due to its extreme bitterness. However, lots of dishes can be flavored with its oil, peel, or zest. Earl Grey tea, for instance, owes its unmistakable aroma to bergamot essential oil, which is also used to add flavor to certain liqueurs, cocktails, and citrus drinks. Bergamot oil and peel are used by upscale restaurants and fans of experimental cuisine to refine the taste of jams, cakes, ice cream, and sorbets. Bergamot oil is particularly popular in the perfume industry as a base fragrance. There is hardly a fresh-smelling aftershave or eau de toilette that does not contain this lemon-like scent.

Cardamom

Origins and cultivation

It is clear from historical accounts by ancient Greek and Roman historians that this spice was known long before the birth of Christ. The plant originally comes from India, and possibly also Sri Lanka. Today cardamom (*Elettaria cardamomum*) is cultivated mainly in South America, in particular in Guatemala. Cardamom is a shrub-like plant that can grow up to 10 feet (3 meters) high and belongs to the ginger family. The plant forms bunchy inflorescences that grow from tripartite, almost triangular, pods. These pods are picked when they are still green—before they are fully ripened—and dried in the sun. The intensely spiced seeds pack in lots of flavor. After saffron and vanilla, cardamom is one of the most expensive and highly prized spices available.

Use

If you open the green, closed pods just before you need to use the cardamom and crush the small, highly aromatic grains in a mortar, the full, sweetish-sharp smell—which is slightly reminiscent of lemon and aniseed—is particularly intense. You can also buy ground cardamom, but often the fruit pod itself has also been ground along with the grains to make this product. Because cardamom keeps its flavor for only a short time, it is better to grind the seeds yourself. Cardamom is predominantly used in oriental and Indian cuisine. As such, it is a classic ingredient in many sophisticated curries. In Germany cardamom is popular in sweet treats that are traditionally baked at Christmas time, but it is also used in various sausage and pie spice mixes. In the Middle East coffee is often spiced with ground cardamom seeds, a tradition espoused by coffee-lovers in other countries, too.

Rosemary

Origins and history

The rosemary bush (*Rosmarinus officinalis*) is an evergreen shrub from the mint family that is endemic to the Mediterranean region. It can grow up to 6½ feet (2 meters) high. The plant enjoyed immense popularity in the ancient world, and the Romans used it to decorate their family altars. Rosemary was dedicated to the goddess Venus. It continued to be prized in the Middle Ages. Many magical properties were ascribed to rosemary: it was said to make people happy, lucky, and rich; to guard against bad dreams; and to prolong youth. Today we are much more matter-of-fact about it, and simply delight in its herbal taste, which gives many dishes their typically Mediterranean flavor.

Cultivation

Rosemary is grown on plantations in many Mediterranean countries. It reproduces through the splitting of the rootstock (vegetative reproduction). The young sprigs are harvested together with their needle-shape leaves.

Use

Rosemary is used a lot in Mediterranean cuisine, either fresh or dried. It is rubbed into meat and fish, or cooked with vegetables and pasta. It is also one of the main components of the hugely popular "herbes de Provence," as well as a tried and tested barbecue seasoning—which should be added to the meat shortly before the end of the grilling process. Rosemary is even used in sweet dishes: the flavor of apple jelly, for instance, can be enhanced by rosemary to wonderful effect. Another connoisseurs' tip for dessert is rosemary ice cream.

Fennel

Origins and cultivation

Not only is fennel (*Foeniculum vulgare*) a well-known vegetable, but its seeds are also used as a spice and healing remedy. Originally a Mediterranean plant, it has since spread all over the world. It is an herbaceous plant and grows to approximately 5 feet (1.5 meters) tall. In Europe fennel is cultivated predominantly in France, Germany, Italy, and Poland. The biennial crop plant prefers warm temperatures. It is grown in many other parts of the world, too. The seed fruits ripen at different speeds, so separating ripe fennel seeds from those that are still developing is a labor-intensive process. The spice is relatively expensive as a result.

History

Fennel was very popular amongst the Romans, who attributed many healing powers to it. From ancient times, the Chinese used fennel in traditional remedies. Fennel continues to be much used in folk medicine, and it has proven antibacterial effects. It is thought to relieve indigestion and help with respiratory disorders, and fennel essential oil is a key ingredient in many cough sweets.

Use

Fennel seeds and spice blends containing fennel are often used as seasonings for fish. In addition, fennel seeds can be used to enhance heavy dishes such as roast potatoes or bratwurst, and to add flavor to sauces and mayonnaise. Like aniseed and caraway, fennel seeds are traditional bread seasonings. As a baking spice, fennel seeds are used especially in spiced cakes and gingerbread. The freshly picked leaves and flower umbels of the fennel plant are, together with fresh dill, ideal for preserving gherkins and pickles.

Star anise

Origins and cultivation

Star anise (*Illicum verum*) comes from an evergreen tree that grows up to 65 feet (20 meters) tall and thrives in the tropics. It is thought to have originated from southern China, the Philippines, and Indonesia. Nowadays the main exporters are China, Vietnam, Thailand, the Philippines, and some Caribbean countries. The star-shape fruit is harvested when it is completely ripe, and is a pericarp consisting of up to eight individual fruits that each harbor a glossy seed. It is always harvested by hand. To make the final product, the fruits are dried in the sun or in drying kilns after being picked.

History

Star anise was hugely popular as a spice in China before the birth of Christ. It is not clear who first brought the spice to Europe. Some sources name Sir Thomas Cavendish, an English privateer and circumnavigator, as the person who first imported star anise, bringing it back from the Philippines on his first voyage round the world (1586–1588). We first find a description of this spice in the records of Carolus Clusius, also known as Charles de l'Ecluse (1526–1609), a botanist who described and cataloged many plant species in writings that have been preserved to this day.

Use

Star anise is sold whole or as a ground spice. It is often used to flavor plum butter, stewed fruit, and baked goods, especially sweet treats at Christmas time, and as one of the spices in mulled wine. Star anise also makes a frequent appearance in Indian curry spice blends. It gives some Chinese standards, such as Peking duck, their distinctive flavor, which can be likened to licorice and aniseed.

Thyme

Origins and history

The thyme genus covers many species, but only common thyme (*Thymus vulgaris*) is used in cooking. Thyme is endemic to the Mediterranean region, but these days is also cultivated in many European countries and in North America. It has long been used both as a herb and as a remedy. The famous Greek physician, pharmacologist, and scholar Pedanios Dioscorides described thyme back in the 1st century AD in his *Materia Medica*. To this day, thyme continues to be used in folk medicine as an effective expectorant for lingering coughs.

Cultivation

Today thyme is grown in temperate regions all over the world. The main producers are Egypt, and in Europe Romania, Bulgaria, and France. The young shoots are harvested; to make dried herbs, they are dried in the sun or in kilns, and then de-stemmed, sifted, and finally packed into bags or pressed into balls and exported. Small common thyme plants can be grown in your own herb garden. They are hardy and recover even from hard frosts in winter if the following spring is mild.

Use

Whether fresh or dried, thyme is a universal herb that is particularly prevalent in Mediterranean cuisine. It is ideal for seasoning vegetable, meat, and fish dishes and can be found in many Mediterranean herb blends, such as the famous "herbes de Provence." Its intensely aromatic yet slightly tart taste also makes it a good addition to herb butters.

Licorice

Origins and cultivation

Licorice root (*Glycyrrhiza glabra*) originally came comes from southern Europe, Anatolia, and the Middle East. It belongs to the Papilionaceae family (legumes). The plant is a perennial and grows up to 5 feet (1.5 meters) high. Licorice as we know it is derived from the plant's strong rootstock. The crop is harvested in its third year by taking the underground stem and shoots, which are sold completely dried or peeled. Licorice is grown in plantations in southern Russia, Ukraine, Spain, and Turkey.

History

The manifold medical properties of licorice root have been known since ancient times. The Egyptians produced a healing drink from licorice infusions. Several centuries before the birth of Christ, the Greeks were using licorice as a remedy for colds. In Europe, licorice and licorice root have been used for their healing properties since the Middle Ages. In 1760 an English apothecary mixed licorice extract with sugar, thus producing sweet licorice, which is still sold in a number of forms by confectioners.

Use

Licorice can be used to give gravies a special flavor—simply put whole licorice sticks in water, bring to the boil, leave to stand for a short time, and then use the intensely flavored broth with the meat juices. Licorice can also be ground into sweet dishes or used in baked goods. To make licorice in the form in which it is sold, the dried root parts are boiled and the liquid thickened until a black mass forms. This kind of licorice can be used in sweet treats and desserts. Licorice has antibacterial, expectorant, and anti-inflammatory effects. Due to its side effects, however, it should never be used for self-medication without the advice of a doctor.

Sage

Origins and cultivation

Sage (*Salvia officinalis*) belongs to the mint family. There are over 800 different varieties, all of which occur in warm to moderate climate zones. However, only the *Salvia officinalis* variety is used as a culinary herb and medicinal plant. This species was originally endemic to the stretch of land between the Dalmatian coast and Macedonia. Today the plant grows all over the Mediterranean region. It is mainly exported by Croatia, Macedonia, and Turkey, where the plant is gathered from the wild, but also cultivated in plantations. Croatia is home to large swathes of wild-growing sage at heights of up to 4,500 feet (1,500 meters) and on offshore islands, especially Pag, where sage is mainly used as feed for milk-producing sheep. Paski sir, a sheep's milk cheese highly prized by foodies, owes its distinctive flavor to this herb.

History

Sage was first known as a medicinal herb. Back in the early Middle Ages, writings from the School of Salerno, one of the medical colleges—with a hospital run by the Benedictine monastery of Monte Cassino—reveal how highly prized sage was at that time. In old books we find the question: "Why should a man die, if there is sage growing in the garden?" To this day, sage is used in all sorts of home remedies, including using a fresh sage leaf to clean teeth and gums. An infusion with hot milk is believed to alleviate colds and sore throats.

Use

We tend to use dried, cut, or uncut sage leaves to flavor meat, in particular roast lamb and pan-fried fish. Sage can also be used in baked goods. A south Tyrolean specialty, for instance, is fresh sage leaves rolled in sweet short pastry, so that after it has been cooked the leaf stalks stick out of the pastry like the tails of mice. Sage is also great for adding flavor to parfaits and ice creams.

Juniper

Origins and cultivation

Juniper (*Juniperus communis*) belongs to the cypress family and is found in moderate climate zones throughout the northern hemisphere. Juniper is dioecious, meaning that there are male and female trees. Male trees bloom with small flowers that are reminiscent of catkins. The female trees grow the juniper berries, although in a strictly botanical sense these are not berries but berry cones. Juniper berries need two years to ripen to maturity. In the first year they are green, and only in the second year do they take on their familiar blueish-black color. There are many different species and subspecies of the juniper family. The main areas that export it are Serbia, Croatia, Macedonia, and other countries in the Balkans.

Use

In cooking, juniper berries are an essential ingredient in sauerkraut and marinades for fish, game dishes, and fatty meats. Juniper's essential oil and the tannins and resins that it contains provide its typical "forest flavor" and make food more wholesome. Juniper is one of the key flavorings in the production of gin, Steinhäger, and genever. Its powerful medicinal effect was known to Sebastian Kneipp (1821–1897), a priest who invented what became known as the Kneipp Cure, whereby one would chew a berry thoroughly on an empty stomach, adding one more berry every morning until the fifteenth day, and then decreasing the number of berries by one a day every day. This treatment is thought to purify the blood and helps to ease gout and rheumatic diseases. However, since the berry is a very a strong irritant to the kidneys, it should be used only in consultation with a doctor.

Marinated salmon with orange and coriander   Serves 6–8

2 oranges
generous ½ cup (160 g) rough sea salt
¾ cup (160 g) sugar
2 tbsp CORIANDER SEEDS
3¼ lb (1.5 kg) salmon, skin on
3½ tbsp gin
1 bunch of fennel fronds
2 lemons

Line a large baking sheet with plastic wrap. The wrap should come over the edges of the baking sheet. Grate the peel from the oranges and squeeze out 3½ tablespoons of orange juice.

Mix the salt, sugar, orange peel, and coriander seeds together. Spread half of the mixture over the baking sheet. Place the fish on top and cover with the rest of the salt mixture. Pour over the orange juice and gin and wrap tightly with the plastic film. Place a board on top of the wrapped fish and weight it down.

Leave in a cool place to marinate for two days, then remove it from the plastic wrap and cut into very thin slices. Serve with the fennel fronds and lemon slices.

A salad and crispbread or pull-apart bread would go well with this dish.

Savory cheesecake

For the pastry
generous 1 cup (150 g) flour
pinch of fleur de sel
1 tbsp THYME
⅓ cup (75 g) butter
baking beans for blind-baking the pastry

For the filling
1 cup (100 g) goat's milk gouda, grated
zest of 1 lemon
2¼ cups (500 g) soft goat's milk cheese
2¼ cups (500 g) quark (40 % fat)
2 tbsp olive oil
1 tbsp ROSEMARY
2 eggs
salt, pepper
fresh herbs to garnish, e.g. cress,
   nasturtiums, borage, basil

Combine the flour, salt, thyme, and butter until the mixture has the consistency of breadcrumbs. Add 1 to 2 tablespoons of ice-cold water and press the mixture onto the base of a 10-inch (26-cm) spring-form tin. Leave it in the refrigerator for approx. 1 hour.

Pre-heat the oven to 390 °F (200 °C). Prick the base several times with a fork, cover with baking parchment, and weight down with the baking beans. Blind-bake in the pre-heated oven for approx. 15 minutes, then take out and leave to cool briefly.

Meanwhile, make the filling by mixing the goat's milk gouda with the lemon zest, soft goat's milk cheese, quark, olive oil, and rosemary. Beat the eggs and mix them in. Season with salt and pepper and spread the mixture over the pre-baked base.

Bake the cheesecake for approx. 1 hour in the fan oven at 300 °F (150 °C). Take it out and leave it to cool completely, then remove it carefully from the spring-form tin. Tear the herbs and scatter over the cheesecake.

A green salad or juicy tomato salad would make a good accompaniment.

Duck rillettes à l'orange

Serves 6–8

Place the duck legs in a heavy-bottomed pot and brown them, skin side down, for approx. 15 minutes over medium heat. Pour off and reserve the fat.

Add the white wine, thyme, bay leaves, peppercorns, juniper berries, and allspice berries to the duck legs and simmer everything over low heat for approx. 3 hours.

Take the duck legs out of the pot. Leave to cool a little and then strip the meat from the bones. Remove the skin, tendons, and cartilage.

Warm the reserved duck cooking fat with the duck lard, add most of the orange zest and leave to infuse over low heat for 10 minutes.

Tear the meat into small pieces. To ensure that the meat and fat are well mixed, put a large metal bowl on ice and mix the meat and warm fat thoroughly within it. A little duck stock can be added if you wish. Garnish with the rest of the orange zest and keep in the refrigerator for 1 day.

Fresh French bread and a green salad go well with duck rillettes.

2¼ lb (1 kg) duck legs
1 quart (1 liter) white wine
1 tbsp **THYME**
3 bay leaves
5 black peppercorns
10 **JUNIPER BERRIES**
10 allspice berries
zest of 1 orange
1 cup (100 g) duck lard
duck stock (optional)

Chicory and pear salad with dark rye bread croutons

Mix the vinegar, buttermilk, licorice, salt, and pepper together to make a dressing. Stir in the oil.

To make the salad, remove the crust from the dark rye bread and cut it into cubes. Put some olive oil in a pan and fry the bread cubes over medium heat until slightly crispy, then add salt, remove them from the pan, and dry off on kitchen paper.

Wash and clean the chicory. Wash the pear, cut into quarters, remove the cores, and cut lengthways into narrow spears. Arrange the chicory leaves and pear spears on plates and drizzle over the dressing. Crumble the cheese and scatter over the salad along with the bread croutons.

For the dressing
1 tbsp white wine vinegar
7 tbsp buttermilk
1 tsp **LICORICE** syrup
or ½ tsp **LICORICE** powder
salt, pepper
3 tbsp oil

For the salad
3 slices of dark rye bread
2 tbsp olive oil
1⅓ cups (400 g) chicory
1 pear
⅔ cup (150 g) soft goat's milk cheese

Fennel soup with star anise oil

For the star anise oil
7 tbsp olive oil
6 **STAR ANISES**

For the fennel soup
1¼ lb (600 g) fennel bulbs
1 cup (100 g) shallots, roughly chopped
generous 1 cup (60 g) potatoes, diced
1 orange
3 tbsp olive oil
3½ cups (800 ml) hot vegetable stock
7 tbsp white wine
1 tsp **FENNEL SEEDS**
1 tsp **CORIANDER SEEDS**
¼ cup (60 ml) aniseed brandy
salt, pepper

Tip

*Any excess star anise oil will keep for
approx. 2 months if stored in a dark place.*

To make the star anise oil, heat the olive oil gently with the star anise, leave to stand for 2 hours, and then strain through a sieve.

For the soup, cut the fennel bulbs into small pieces and place the green parts to one side.

Heat the olive oil in a large pot. Sauté the roughly chopped shallots until they are translucent.

Add the fennel pieces and the diced potato, and continue to cook.

Grate the zest of the orange and squeeze out the juice.

Add the hot stock, white wine, fennel seeds, coriander seeds, and orange juice. Cover the pot and leave to boil gently over medium heat for 20 minutes.

Purée the soup and add aniseed brandy, 1 tablespoon of star anise oil, salt, pepper, and orange zest to taste.

You could serve saffron scones (see page 54) with the soup.

Carrot and cardamom soup

1¼ lb (600 g) carrots
2 sticks of celery
1 onion
1 orange
2 tbsp olive oil
1 quart (1 liter) vegetable stock
1 bay leaf
1 tsp **CARDAMOM**
salt

Peel the carrots and cut into small pieces. Cut the celery sticks into strips, and peel and finely chop the onion. Squeeze the orange and reserve the juice.

Sweat the carrot, celery, and onion in the olive oil. Add the stock, orange juice, bay leaf, and cardamom. Leave to simmer for about 20 minutes, until the carrot is soft. Purée the soup using a stick blender and add salt to taste.

Potato and sage pizza Makes 2 pizzas

For the starter dough
⅓ cup (50 g) wheat flour
1½ tbsp water
½ tsp (1 g) fresh yeast

For the main dough
scant ¾ cup (150 g) semolina
⅓ cup (50 g) wheat flour
½ cup (125 g) water
4 tsp olive oil
4 g fresh yeast
1 tsp salt

For the topping
14 oz (400 g) potatoes
2 balls of mozzarella
1 cup (250 g) ricotta
1 tbsp dried **ROSEMARY**
pepper
sea salt
olive oil
handful of fresh **SAGE LEAVES**

Knead the ingredients for the starter dough together and leave overnight.

The next day, knead the starter dough together with the ingredients for the main dough in a food processor for 5 minutes on the lowest setting, and then for 10 to 15 minutes on the second setting until the dough comes away from the bottom of the bowl and looks taut. Cover the dough and leave in the refrigerator for at least 48 hours (maximum 5 to 7 days).

When you are ready to bake the pizzas, divide the dough in two and form two pizza bases.

To make the topping, cut the potatoes into very thin slices using a knife or a plane, and blanch them in boiling salted water for 3 minutes. Slice the ricotta and mozzarella.

Pre-heat the oven to 480 °F (250 °C). Place the ricotta and mozzarella slices over the pizza bases, followed by a layer of the potato slices. Season with rosemary, freshly ground pepper, and sea salt, and drizzle over some olive oil. Bake in the pre-heated oven for approx. 10 to 15 minutes, until the base is crispy and brown.

Meanwhile, deep fry the sage leaves in plenty of olive oil in a pan, and scatter over the pizzas before serving.

Braised leg of lamb with rosemary polenta   Serves 4

Rub the leg of lamb all over with salt and pepper. Peel the sweet potatoes and carrots and cut into sticks. Peel the shallots and garlic. Cut the garlic cloves in half. Cut the lemon peel into strips.

Pre-heat the oven to 355 °F (180 °C). Heat the olive oil in a large ovenproof roasting dish and sear the lamb. Add the sweet potatoes, carrot, shallots, garlic, lemon peel, fresh rosemary, and bay leaves to the dish. Pour in the milk and season with salt and pepper.

Place on the bottom shelf of the pre-heated oven, cover with a lid, and braise for about 80 to 90 minutes. Turn the meat often and spoon over the milk.

While the lamb is cooking, bring the stock to the boil and add the polenta, stirring constantly, then remove from the heat and leave to stand for approx. 10 minutes. Add the crème fraîche and a teaspoon of dried rosemary, and mix. Carve the meat and serve with the polenta.

1 leg of lamb (approx. 4 lb/1.8 kg)
3 sweet potatoes
2 large carrots
6 shallots
1 bulb of garlic
peel of 2 lemons
2 tbsp olive oil
3 sprigs of **ROSEMARY**
8 bay leaves
1⅔ cups (400 ml) milk
3¼ cups (750 ml) vegetable stock
scant 1½ cups (250 g) polenta (cornmeal)
3 tbsp crème fraîche
1 tsp dried **ROSEMARY**
salt, pepper

Pork tenderloin in orange caramel   Serves 4

Grate 1 tablespoon of peel from one of the oranges and squeeze out ½ cup (125 ml) of juice. Put the orange juice, sugar, and orange liqueur in a pot, bring to the boil, and simmer until it thickens slightly.

Rub the pork tenderloin with salt and pepper. Heat the olive oil and brown the tenderloin on all sides until golden brown. Pour in the orange caramel, cover, and braise the meat over low heat for 15 to 20 minutes. Turn the meat every so often.

At 5 minutes before the end of the cooking time, add the grated orange peel. Leave everything to stand. Cut the meat into four slices and serve drizzled with the orange caramel.

2–3 oranges
4 tbsp sugar
4–5 tbsp orange-based liqueur
1¾ lb (800 g) pork tenderloin
2 tbsp olive oil
salt, pepper

Gnocchi with melted tomatoes and star anise Serves 4

7 tbsp (100 g) butter
3 **STAR ANISES**
2¼ lb (1 kg) potatoes
generous 2 cups (300 g) flour
1 egg yolk
1 tsp salt + extra for seasoning
1¾ cups (500 g) multicolored cherry
  tomatoes
pepper
THAI BASIL or **BASIL** to garnish

Melt the butter in a pot, add the star anise, and leave to stand for 30 minutes.

Wash the potatoes thoroughly. Leaving their skins on, boil them in water for 20 to 30 minutes, depending on their size. Drain and remove the peel. Mash the potatoes while they are still hot or put them through a potato ricer. Fold in the flour, egg yolk, and a teaspoon of salt.

Roll the dough out on a floured surface so that it is the same thickness as a finger. Cut it into pillow-like shapes and roll them over a gnocchi board or press a grooved pattern into them using a fork.

Cook the gnocchi for about 3 minutes in plenty of water at a rolling boil, until they rise to the surface. Remove them with a slotted spoon, leave to drain, and keep warm.

Meanwhile, halve the tomatoes and heat them in the star anise butter. Sauté for about 3 minutes and season with salt and pepper. Mix with the gnocchi and serve garnished with the basil.

Zucchini quiche with goat's milk cheese Makes 1 tart

For the pastry
1¾ cups (250 g) flour
1 tsp salt
8½ tbsp (125 g) cold butter

For the filling
4 zucchini (1.5 kg)
2 onions
2 garlic cloves
1 tbsp oil
1 tsp **THYME**
1 tsp **ROSEMARY**
1⅓ cups (300 g) soft goat's milk cheese
3 eggs
grated peel of 1 lemon
salt, pepper

To make the pastry, mix the flour with the salt and add the butter to it in cubes. Work all of the ingredients together until they form a crumbly dough. Add 1 to 2 tablespoons of ice-cold water and knead the dough quickly until it is stretchy. Roll it into a ball with your hands, wrap it in plastic wrap, and leave it in the refrigerator for 30 minutes.

To make the filling, wash the zucchini and cut them into cubes. Peel and finely chop the onions and garlic, and then sauté them in the oil until they are translucent. Sprinkle with thyme and rosemary. Add the zucchini and fry for about 10 to 15 minutes. Leave to cool briefly.

Pre-heat the oven to 390 °F (200 °C). Whisk the cheese with the eggs, and season with salt, pepper, and the lemon peel.

Grease a tart tin. Roll the dough out onto a floured surface that is a little bigger than the tin, and then place it in the tin. Spread the zucchini over the pastry base and pour over the egg-and-cheese mixture. Bake in the pre-heated oven for 30 to 35 minutes until golden brown.

Bergamot pavlova with tangerine and lemon curd and persimmons

Pre-heat the oven to 210 °F (100 °C). To make the pavlova, beat the egg whites with the salt until they form stiff peaks. Grind the sugar with the Earl Grey or mix it with the bergamot oil and gradually add it to the egg whites.

Add the vinegar and beat again until the sugar has dissolved. Mix the confectioners' sugar together with the cornstarch and sieve it into the beaten egg whites.

Spoon the egg white mixture into a large round pavlova shape on a baking sheet lined with baking parchment and make a well in the middle. Leave it to dry for approx. 90 minutes in the pre-heated oven, with the door slightly open. Remove from the oven and leave to cool.

To make the tangerine and lemon curd, grate the peel of one of the tangerines and squeeze out ⅓ cup (75 ml) of juice. Put the sugar, eggs, egg yolk, tangerine juice and peel, and lemon juice, in a heatproof bowl over a gently simmering double boiler. Do not allow the eggs to congeal.

Remove the bowl of creamy mixture from the double boiler, add the butter, and stir until it melts. Leave the mixture to cool.

Wash the persimmons and cut them into thin slices. Spread the tangerine curd over the pavlova, add the quark over the top, and garnish with the persimmon slices.

For the meringue
2 egg whites
pinch of salt
3½ tbsp (50 g) sugar
2 tsp Earl Grey tea leaves or 1 drop of **BERGAMOT** oil
1 tsp white wine vinegar
7 tbsp (50 g) confectioners' sugar
2 tsp cornstarch

For the tangerine and lemon curd
1–2 tangerines
7 tbsp (100 g) sugar
2 eggs
1 egg yolk
3½ tbsp (50 ml) lemon juice
3½ tbsp (50 g) butter
2 persimmons
1 cup (200 g) cream quark.

A pavlova is a fruit-filled torte on a meringue base.

Orange and cardamom parfait   Serves 4

Grate the peel of 1 orange and squeeze out the juice. Crush the cardamom pods and grind the seeds in a mortar.

Fill a pot with water and bring it to the boil. Beat the egg yolks and sugar in a heatproof dish in a hot double boiler until the mixture is creamy and starts to thicken. Transfer to a cold double boiler and stir until the mixture is cool. Fold in the orange juice, peel, liqueur, and cardamom.

Beat the cream until stiff and fold into the creamy mixture. Divide the parfait between the little tins and freeze for at least 6 hours.

1–2 **ORANGES**
1 tsp **CARDAMOM**
3 egg yolks
5 tbsp (70 g) sugar
3½ tbsp orange-based liqueur
generous 6 tbsp (100 g) whipping cream

Spices with Spirit and Sass:

The Hot Ones

You do not have to go far to experience the taste and, indeed, the benefits of hot spices. Horseradish, which has always been a staple of peasant food and in recent years has become especially popular in vegetarian cuisine, comes both in a mildly flavored and a searingly hot form. The latter helps to ward off colds and has antibacterial properties. Whole regions have traditionally added some pizazz to sausages and prepared medicinal poultices using mustard seeds, and today mustard takes the form of a rich variety of savory condiments. The capsaicin in pepper and chili gives real heat to food, while also releasing happiness hormones. Meanwhile, cloves and ginger are spicy kitchen standards, and can also be used in soothing drinks. Hot herbs and spices provide the spirited backing vocals in the spectacle of today's fusion cuisine.

Chili

Origins and history

Chili peppers are closely related to sweet peppers (*Capsicum* genus), and are amongst the hottest of all the *Capsicum* species. The spice, which when dried and ground is called Cayenne pepper, owes its heat to its high content of capsaicin, an alkaloid. There are varieties that are so hot that even touching them can cause irritation of the skin. Chilies were originally endemic to Central and South America. Grave finds show that chilies were being grown in large plantations in Peru several centuries before the birth of Christ. In the 15th century, Spanish conquistadors in South America began to use this spice as a substitute for pepper and brought it back with them to Europe. Its additional name of pepper probably dates from this time. Nonetheless, from a botanical point of view Cayenne pepper has nothing to do with the pepper plant family.

Cultivation

Chilies are mainly grown in and exported from various countries in Central and South America, Thailand, India, Nigeria, and China. In tropical areas, the chili plant reaches heights of about 3 feet (1 meter). Its small, red fruit, approx. ¾ –1¼ inches (2–3 cm) long, are picked by hand.

Use

Chilies and Cayenne pepper give a markedly peppery heat to any dish. Chilies are used in almost every fish and meat dish in South American cuisine, and they are often a key ingredient in curry spice blends. They are also used in North American cooking, in a spice mix that often goes by the name of chili powder or chili pepper. The main spices in this blend are chilies, cumin, coriander, garlic, and oregano. The capsaicin contained in chilies is also a component of a number of skin ointments; capsaicin acts on the skin's heat receptors, improving circulation and helping to prevent muscle tension and rheumatism.

Garlic

Origins and history

Garlic (*Allium sativum*) belongs to the lily family (Liliaceae). The original wild garlic variety was endemic to the steppes of Asia and is now extinct. Garlic was known to the ancient world: the Greeks and Romans were aware of its healing properties and used it frequently. In the Middle Ages it was grown by monasteries, and it remains a fixture in cottage gardens to this day, while it is popular in cooking and as an ingredient in various remedies.

Cultivation

Today garlic is grown in moderate climate zones all over the world. Its main growing area is China, which caters for almost 80 percent of the global demand. Other supplier areas are California, India, Spain, and some of the Balkan countries.

Use

Garlic is grown and sold in an array of different forms: dried as granules, in flakes, in slices, ground, mixed with salt, or as an ingredient in myriad spice blends. Both Mediterranean and Asian cuisine would be very different without garlic. As a result, garlic has become a firm fixture in almost every cuisine in the world. It gives many different sauces, fish and meat dishes, soups, salads, and vegetable dishes their distinctive flavor. Garlic also plays a starring role in a number of famous dishes, such as the Italian "spaghetti aglio e olio," the Greek tsatsiki, and the Spanish "gambas al ajillo." The medical benefits of garlic are undisputed—it has a strong antibacterial effect, can reduce high blood pressure, and can prevent arteriosclerosis.

Ginger

Origins and distribution

Ginger (*Zingiber officinalis*) belongs to the ginger family (Zingiberacae) and thrives in the tropics and subtropics. It has been known to the Chinese and Indians since ancient times. Arab merchants later brought it to southern Europe. The first known mention of ginger appears in a cookbook by Marcus Gavius Apicius (25 BC – 42 AD), a Roman epicure who ran a number of cooking schools and poured his fortune into producing an elaborate guide to cuisine.

Cultivation

Ginger is cultivated in China, India, Thailand, Nigeria, and South America. These days China is the biggest exporter. It grows as an herbaceous plant that can reach up to 4 feet (1.2 meters) tall. With its leaves and thick stalk, it is similar to reed-like plants. The subsurface rhizome or rootstalk is harvested.

Use

Ginger is sold both fresh and dried, and is especially prevalent in Asian cuisine. Its sharp, hot taste peps up soups, salads, meat and fish dishes, drinks and teas, and even baked goods and various desserts. It can also be used to pickle gherkins and pumpkin, blended into chocolates and pralines, or used as part of sausage seasoning. Last but not least, it tastes delightful when candied. Ginger has antioxidant and anti-inflammatory effects and is used in traditional Chinese medicine to ward off rheumatism and coughs and sneezes.

Cloves

Origins and history

The clove tree (*Syzygium aromaticum*) is an evergreen, tropical tree that is originally endemic to the Moluccas and belongs to the myrtle family. Cloves are obtained from the unopened, dried flower buds. In 1605 the Dutch wrested the Moluccas from Portuguese control, and exporting the seeds or cuttings of the clove tree became punishable by death. Despite this draconian threat, the Dutch monopoly was overturned in 1770 by the French, who managed to smuggle seeds and small cuttings from the clove tree off the islands. A little later, the first plantations were grown on Réunion and Mauritius. Originally, cloves were far more highly prized for their use in medicine than as a spice. Even in ancient times, the Chinese imported cloves as a remedy for toothache, whereby a clove would simply be inserted between the cheek and the affected tooth. Due to their high eugenol content, cloves are still an easy household remedy to give you fresh, pleasant breath—simply swirl a clove round your mouth for about three minutes, chewing it a little if you wish.

Cultivation

Together with the Moluccas, the main suppliers are the Philippines, Sri Lanka, Madagascar, Brazil, and some Caribbean islands.

Use

Today cloves are used to add flavor to sauces, fish and meat dishes, gingerbread and almond cookies, marinades, red cabbage, soups, plum-based dishes, mulled wine, and spice blends. A useful tip for checking the quality of dried cloves is to put them in a glass of water. Good cloves float vertically, while substandard cloves—which have probably lost their oil or are outdated—lie horizontally on the surface of the water.

Espelette pepper

Origins and history

Espelette pepper is the finely ground or pulverized dark red fruit of the eponymous pepper. This type of pepper, which is very hot and closely related to the chili pepper, is grown in the Basque country, but originally came from Central America. The area round Espelette, which lies at the foot of the Pyrenees, is ideal terrain for the pepper due to its microclimate. Even today it is almost exclusively picked by hand.

Cultivation

The small Basque town of Espelette, the center of the growing area for this type of pepper, lies about 25 miles (40 km) from Biarritz. The French Institut national de l'origine et de la qualité has bestowed the designation of origin AOC on Espelette pepper and the spice produced from it in this town and nine surrounding villages. The seedlings grown from the seeds are transplanted from greenhouses to the outdoors in spring each year. The bush-like plant can grow to over 3 feet (1 meter) tall. It is harvested from the end of September to the beginning of November.

Use

Traditionally, Espelette pepper comes in the form of whole, ripe, deep red peppers dried in the sun and strung decoratively on thin cords in shops. The dried peppers, ground or coarsely crushed to form Espelette pepper, are prized by foodies and professional chefs for their hotness and full-bodied taste. Espelette pepper is the main flavoring ingredient in typical Basque dishes such as piperade, which combines tomatoes and scrambled eggs. In addition, Espelette pepper can be used in any dish in which you would normally use chilies or pepper. In the Basque country the spice is also found in bread dough, mustard, cheese, and even chocolate.

Mustard seeds

Origins and history

A distinction is drawn between yellow or white mustard (*Sinapsis alba*) and the somewhat hotter black or brown mustard (*Brassica nigra*). Mustard was known in China as early as several thousand years ago. It first reached Greece, and later the Romans, by way of Asia Minor. At this time mustard and horseradish were the only hot spices available to cooks. It is thought that Lucius Lunius Moderatus Columella, who was born in Spain and later lived near Rome, was the first to publish a recipe for making mustard, in 42 BC. This sparked an increase in the use of mustard seeds and table mustard, to the point where they now play an important role in our cuisine.

Cultivation

Today mustard is cultivated in fields across central and southern Europe.

Use

Mustard seeds are mainly used in the production of table mustard and mustard powder. In the West we mainly use the white or yellow type of mustard, while in India people prefer the black mustard seeds, for instance in curries. Mustard seeds, which have a strong preservative effect, are used to flavor pickled gherkins, mustard fruits, and sweet and sour vegetables; and in mixed pickles, marinades for fish, sauerkraut, and sauces. Mustard is also used for sausage seasoning. Mustard powder and mustard flour can also be used directly in cooking, for example in soups and sauces, although mustard flour is primarily used to produce table mustard. When combined with other spices, salt, vinegar, wine, and sugar, it results in products with a wide range of flavors.

Mountain pepper

Origins and cultivation

Mountain pepper (*Tasmannia lanceolata*), also known as Tasmanian pepperberry, mostly occurs in Australia, and Tasmania in particular. It thrives best in warm, damp rainforests, where it grows in bush form and can reach up to 10 feet (3 meters) tall. British settlers discovered the pepperiness of its wrinkled little fruits and used them to add flavor to meat. Later it was exported to Great Britain. To this day, it is prevalent in the cuisine of Cornwall, where an acclimatized form of Tasmanian pepper is cultivated, and cooks use not only the burningly hot fruits, but also the dried leaves, finely ground, as a spice. It is known in the UK as Cornish pepperleaf.

Use

Although mountain pepper is not related the black pepper, it is used in exactly the same way. However, mountain pepper is much hotter, so unless you are used to it, add it sparingly.

Sichuan pepper

Origins and cultivation

Although it has the word "pepper" in its name, botanically speaking Sichuan pepper has nothing to do with the black pepper plant family (*Piper nigrum*). And it has still less in common with other spices that have pepper in their name simply because they are peppery and acrid, despite coming from other plant families—such as Malagueta pepper, pink pepper, and mountain pepper. Sichuan pepper (*Zanthoxylum piperitum*) belongs to the rue family and is related to citrus species. The name comes from the Chinese province of Sichuan, where—as in Korea, Japan, and Tibet—it grows in the wild and is also cultivated in plantations. In its homeland it grows as a perennial shrub, reaching about 6½ feet (2 meters). It also thrives in gardens in temperate climes.

Use

Both the dried seed capsules of Sichuan pepper, which constitute the spice itself, and its fresh leaves make excellent seasoning for dishes from Far East Asia. You have to accustom yourself to the taste a little: amides, chemical compounds based on ammonia, initially cause a tingling sensation and then a slightly numbing effect on the lips and tongue. Sichuan pepper is used in dishes such as fiery Sichuan beef, and in hot Chinese sauces. It is also used in Asian spice blends.

Horseradish

Origins and cultivation

Horseradish originally came from southeastern Europe and western Asia. In the wake of the migration period, it also became native to central Europe. Since then, it has spread to northern Europe and North America, and also occurs growing in the wild in these regions. Horseradish (*Armoracia rusticana*) belongs to the mustard family and is a herbaceous plant that can grow to 3 feet (1 meter) tall. The large and sturdy tap root can be used as a spice and is harvested by digging it up, even well into a mild winter. The washed and scrubbed root is put in cold storage at 28 to 23 °F (–2 to –5 °C) and will keep for a long time.
Horseradish is propagated solely by using its rhizomes. The pencil-thick root cuttings are stored in damp sand over a frost-free winter and then, in early spring, are planted into soft, prepared soil. The roots can be harvested in the second or third year.

Use

The distinctive, sharp taste that immediately hits the nose and tongue is due to allyl mustard oil. Grated horseradish goes with roast beef, fish, stewed beef, and chicken salad. Grated horseradish is also found in specialty mustards. It is believed to have a strong antimicrobial and antiviral effect.

Allspice

Origins and history

Christopher Columbus, who discovered America in 1492, is said to have brought the first allspice berries back to Europe from Jamaica. The late 17th century saw the use of allspice really begin to take off, especially in England. Due to its origins, allspice is also known as Jamaica pepper or newspice (i.e. from the New World), but the name "allspice" has stuck because the berries seem to combine lots of flavors of other spices in one (cinnamon, nutmeg, cloves, pepper).

Cultivation

Jamaica remains one of the major exporters of this spice, followed by Mexico, Grenada, Guatemala, and Brazil. Allspice (*Pimenta officinalis*) belongs to the myrtle family. Its tree grows up to 32 feet (10 meters) tall and has dark green, leathery, wide and lance-shape leaves. The fruits are picked when they are still green and unripe. When they become ripe and then red, the fruits lose their value as a spice as they hardly have any essential oil left and lose their flavor. When dried in the sun, the green, unripe fruits acquire their familiar dark brown color.

Use

Whole allspice corns are an ingredient in many marinades (e.g. for classic braised beef), and they can also be used to wonderful effect in desserts. The spiced biscuits traditionally made in the run-up to Christmas would be unimaginable without allspice, and it is also a vital part of all sorts of spice mixes for Middle Eastern and Indian cuisine. Allspice is used to season game and to complement pickled food. Ground allspice is used in baked goods, in particular gingerbread, and in sausage seasoning (e.g. for black pudding), liqueurs, and even chocolate. In the Caribbean the fresh green leaves of the allspice tree are used for adding flavor to fish soups, stews, and the cooking water for crustaceans.

Spotlight on Mustard: A Gift from the Romans

The seeds of three different mustard plants are used to produce mustard: white mustard (*Brassica alba*), black mustard (*Brassica nigra*), and brown mustard (*Brassica juncea*). These all belong to the mustard family and are closely related to radish and rapeseed.

The mustard plant has been known in China for 3,000 years and was used variously as a medicinal and spice plant. In the ancient world, the Romans, Egyptians, and Greeks were also familiar with mustard. Through the Romans, the use of mustard spread throughout central and southern Europe, and soon caught on as an easy way of pepping up food.

Mustard's innocuous-looking, almost odorless seeds contain all their hotness within. When you first bite into one, there is a noticeable mildly nutty flavor. The glycoside sinalbin and the enzyme myrosinase then take effect, releasing their sharp taste.

To make mustard, white, brown, and black mustard seeds are mixed with one another in different ratios, as required by the recipe, and then ground. Traditionally, grape juice is added to this mustard flour. Besides water, the other basic ingredients in mustard are vinegar, salt, and—depending on the type of mustard—other spices. The distinctive flavor emerges when it is put in vats and the mash formed by the ingredients is left to ferment.

The substances contained in mustard seeds and the ingredients used in the production of the end product (acid and salt) are sufficient to preserve it. However, it is worth looking out for organic varieties of mustard, which do not contain any artificial acidifying agents or antioxidants.

Different production methods result in different types of mustard. The degree to which the mustard seeds are ground down and the proportions of white, black, and brown mustard and the other ingredients and spices used mean there is a vast array of different mustard products.

Deli-style or medium-hot mustard is made from white and brown mustard seeds. Adding horseradish makes horseradish mustard, which is particularly hot.

Hot mustard is made by adding a greater proportion of brown mustard seeds. Sweet mustard uses white and brown mustard seeds that are slightly toasted. The sweetness comes from the addition of sugar and sweeteners or apple purée. Honey also features in a number of especially upscale products.

For rôtisseur mustard the seeds are ground coarsely, so that the mustard is less sensitive to heat and can be used as a marinade for grilling and roasting. Dijon mustard originally comes from the French town of Dijon, which had a monopoly on mustard-making in the 13th century. Today there is no longer a single mustard factory in the town. Dijon mustard does not have a protected designation of origin, but is simply made according to a recipe that was devised in 18th-century Dijon.

Mustard powder, which is particularly popular in England, is made from ground mustard flour and various herbs and spices. Pure ground mustard is found in many curry mixes.

Spotlight on Salt

Salt has been an indispensable ingredient in cooking throughout the history of mankind. The Sumerians and Babylonians used it to preserve meat and vegetables. Strictly speaking, salt is not a spice, as officially spices are made from parts of plants. Nevertheless, it is the most important condiment of them all. Used sparingly, it can define and enhance the taste of individual foods or prepared dishes. Yet salts are not all the same. Indeed, there are four main kinds in use.

Everyday cooking salt, which can be bought in supermarkets, has undergone a chemical refining process that removes almost all of the main trace elements and minerals such as calcium, iron, and zinc. Magnesium carbonate and other flow additives are added to improve its pourability.

Sea salt is obtained from salt evaporation ponds. The salt content of seawater is approximately 3.5 percent, so 1 quart (1 liter) of seawater contains 1¼ ounces (35 g) of salt. The seawater is channeled into shallow pools, where an intense evaporation process takes place through exposure to the sun and wind. This greatly increases the concentration of salt in the remaining water. The concentrated brine is then channeled into other pools, until the salt on the bottom of the pools crystallizes. This salt contains more than just sodium chloride—it also has potassium, magnesium, and the trace element manganese. Lots of cooks prefer to use sea salt because of its superior taste, although, like other kinds of salt, its sodium chloride content is 95–98 percent, and whether it actually tastes different to cooking salt is a matter of fierce debate. One interesting type of sea salt is fleur de sel, or *flor de sal* in Spanish. This comes from the ultra-thin layer of salt that forms on the surface of the drying pools when it is very hot and the air is calm, and is then painstakingly skimmed off by hand. Fleur de sel is sold in its natural and unwashed state. The magnesium sulfate present in this type of salt gives it a slightly bitter taste. Fleur de sel is especially popular amongst gourmands.

Rock salt is a mineral extracted from salt mines. It was formed millions of years ago when the ancient seas dried out.

Himalayan salt is another type of rock salt, extracted by miners. It is more than 97 percent sodium chloride, and its distinctive pink hue is caused by its low level of iron oxide compounds. It is mined in Pakistan, about 150 miles (250 km) from the spurs of the Himalayas. The Pakistan salt mine has existed for over 400 years. The health benefits ascribed to this type of salt have not yet been proved.

A number of other products also lure customers in with terms such as "original salt." This tends to be mined rock salt, which often comes untreated and in large flakes. Boasting that such salt comes from salt beds that are 200 million years old does not carry any weight: many salt deposits are as old or older.

Evaporated salt is extracted through drill holes in a layer of stone, and is used for cooking salt. Groundwater is piped through the drill holes. The resulting brine is pumped out, and the salt is then obtained by evaporating the brine in large evaporation pans.

Spicy olives Serves 4

generous 1 lb (500 g) olives
½ tsp CUMIN
½ tsp coriander seeds
½ tsp peppercorns
1 red CHILI
4 GARLIC CLOVES
grated peel of ½ orange
2 sprigs of rosemary
generous ¾ cup (200 ml) olive oil

Wash and dry the olives, and then put them in a large jar. Toast the cumin and coriander briefly in a pan and then crush them roughly in a mortar together with the peppercorns.

Cut the chili into fine rings, and peel and chop the garlic.

Add the spices and the rest of the ingredients to the jar and leave to stand in the refrigerator for a month.

Harissa Makes 2 jars (7 oz/200 ml each)

1¾ oz (50 g) hot CHILIES
1 can of peeled tomatoes (9 oz/250 g)
2 large GARLIC CLOVES
2 or 3 shallots, finely chopped
½ tsp caraway
1 tsp cumin seeds
1 tsp coriander seeds
½ tsp salt
3½ tbsp olive oil + extra as required

De-seed and roughly chop the chilies. Ideally, wear disposable gloves as the chilies are likely to make your skin smart.

Put the tomatoes, chilies, and the rest of the ingredients in a small pot, and bring it to the boil. Leave to simmer for about 10 minutes, until the mixture has thickened a little. Leave to cool.

Purée until smooth with a handheld blender, and then pour the mixture into pre-warmed, sterilized jars until it is 1/2 inch (1 cm) under the rim. Top up with oil and seal the jars.

If kept in the fridge, the harissa will keep for 4 months.

Plantain chips Serves 4

4 plantains
4 tbsp coconut oil
½ tsp hot SMOKED PAPRIKA
salt

Pre-heat the oven to 390 °F (200 °C) and line a baking sheet with baking parchment.

Score down the plantains lengthways and carefully peel them using your hands or a knife. Cut them into thin slices (about the thickness of a coin) using a mandolin or a sharp knife.

Melt the coconut oil and mix with the plantains and smoked paprika in a bowl. Place the chips on the prepared baking sheet and bake for approx. 30 minutes in the oven. Take them out and sprinkle them with salt.

Hot salmon ceviche in coconut milk Serves 4

Cut the salmon into very small cubes. Pour over the lime juice, mix well, and leave to marinate for 15 minutes.

Chop the shallot and chili very finely and add to the salmon together with the oil, ginger, coconut milk, and ground cloves. Mix well once again.

Season with fleur de sel and pepper and serve immediately. This goes well with crunchy plantain chips (see page 104).

1¼ lb (600 g) skinless salmon
juice and zest of 2 limes
1 shallot
1 red **CHILI**
3 tbsp olive oil
½ tbsp chopped **GINGER**
7 tbsp coconut milk
½ tsp **GROUND CLOVES**
2 tsp fleur de sel
pepper

Burrata with cherries and pepper Serves 4

Wash, pit, and halve the cherries. Mix the olive oil and cherry vinegar together thoroughly and season with salt and pepper. Add the cherries and leave to marinate for about 20 minutes.

Wash the rocket and pat dry. Toast the almonds in a dry pan and then chop them roughly. Drain the burrata and cut each of the balls in half.

Divide the rocket, burrata, and cherries between 4 plates, garnish with the almonds, and grind some pepper over the top.

generous 1 cup (200 g) cherries
3 tbsp olive oil
2 tbsp sour cherry vinegar or red wine vinegar
7 cups (200 g) rocket, packed
2 tbsp almonds
2 balls of burrata
salt
RED, **BLACK**, and **SICHUAN PEPPER**

Fish parcels with ginger Serves 4

4 fish fillets, e.g. cod
4 scallions
generous 1 lb (500 g) snow peas
2-inch (5-cm) piece of **GINGER**
3 tbsp olive oil
1 lemon
salt, pepper

Wash the fish and pat dry. Pre-heat the oven to 355 °F (180 °C). Wash and slice the scallions. Wash the snow peas and cut them in half. Peel and finely chop the ginger.

Divide the vegetables and ginger between 4 pieces of baking parchment. Place a fish fillet on top of each and drizzle with olive oil. Season with salt and pepper. Cut the lemon into slices and place them on top of the fish.

Pull the paper up round the fish, scrunch the sides so that the parcels look like sweets, and tie them firmly closed with cooking string. Bake the fish parcels in the oven for about 12 to 15 minutes.

Fillet of beef with chimichurri Serves 4

generous 1 lb (500 g) baby new potatoes
fleur de sel
2 tbsp olive oil
2¼ lb (1 kg) fillet of beef
2 tbsp butter
pepper

For the chimichurri
2 **GARLIC CLOVES**
1 onion
1 bunch of parsley
1 tbsp fresh thyme needles
1 tsp **CHILI**, chopped
½ tsp sea salt
pepper
3 tbsp olive oil
2 tbsp white wine vinegar

Pre-heat the oven to 390 °F (200 °C). Line a baking sheet with baking parchment. Wash the potatoes, cut into quarters, place on the baking sheet, and sprinkle with fleur de sel, pepper, and olive oil, turning the potato pieces so that they are well covered. Make sure that they are evenly spaced and then bake them in the pre-heated oven for about 35 to 40 minutes.

Rub the fillet of beef with fleur de sel and pepper. Warm the butter in the roasting dish and sear the meat on all sides. Place the fillet of beef on top of the potatoes and cook for about 30 minutes. Once the core temperature reaches 140 °F (60 °C), the beef is medium done.

To make the chimichurri, peel and finely chop the garlic and onion. Chop the parsley and pound it in a mortar with the thyme, chili, salt, and pepper.

All the oil and vinegar to the herbs and mix until the sauce is smooth. Leave it to stand for about 20 minutes.

Take the beef and potatoes out of the oven, cover with aluminum foil, and leave to stand for 5 to 10 minutes. Then cut up the meat and serves with the rosemary potatoes and the chimichurri.

Rabbit in tarragon and mustard sauce Serves 4

Pre-heat the oven to 355 °F (180 °C). Wash the rabbit pieces and pat dry. Season with salt and pepper.

Heat the oil in a stew pot and sear the rabbit pieces on both sides for 2 to 3 minutes.

Peel and finely chop the shallots, and add to the meat along with the mustard seeds, wine, and chicken stock. Braise for approx. 2 hours in the oven, basting often with the roasting juices.

When the cooking time is almost finished, chop the tarragon leaves finely. Remove the rabbit pieces from the broth and keep them warm. Transfer the pot to the stove and boil the stock down until it is about half of its original volume.

Stir the crème fraîche, mustard, and tarragon into the rabbit stock and bring to the boil. Season to taste with salt and pepper. Pour the mustard sauce over the rabbit and serve with potatoes.

1 rabbit (ask your butcher to divide it up)
salt, pepper
4 tbsp olive oil
4 shallots
1 tsp **MUSTARD SEEDS**
1⅔ cups (400 ml) white wine
generous ¾ cup (200 ml) chicken stock
1 bunch of tarragon
generous ¾ cup (200 g) crème fraîche
3 tbsp **MUSTARD**

Lentil and goat's milk cheese salad with mustard dressing Serves 4

Rinse the lentils under cold water, then put them in a pot with lots of water, bring to the boil, drain, and simmer over low heat for about 35 minutes in approx. 1 quart (1 liter) of water. Drain in a sieve.

Wash the tomatoes and cut into quarters. Mix the mustard, vinegar, olive oil, salt, and pepper to form a sauce and pour it over the drained lentils.

Cut the cheeses into 8 slices and place them on a baking sheet lined with baking parchment. Toast them under a hot grill or on the highest shelf of the oven until their tops are brown.

Divide the lentils between 4 plates and garnish with the tomatoes and goat's milk cheese.

scant 1½ cups (300 g) Puy lentils
1½ cups (400 g) cherry tomatoes
2 tsp **MUSTARD**
4 tbsp white wine vinegar
4 tbsp olive oil
2 rolls of soft goat's milk cheese
    (5½ oz/150 g each)
salt, pepper

Spicy grilled octopus salad Serves 4

2¼ lb (1 kg) octopus
1 onion
1 carrot
2 garlic cloves
1 bay leaf
2 avocados
generous 1 cup (250 g) cherry tomatoes
½ bunch parsley
1 lemon
½ tsp **CHILI FLAKES**
1 tsp rosemary
4 tbsp olive oil
salt

Rinse the octopus under cold, running water, leave to dry, and then tenderize it with a meat mallet. Cut the tentacles from the body and press out the beak.

Fill a large pot with salted water and bring it to the boil. Peel the onion and cut it into quarters. Cut the carrot into thick slices. Peel and halve one of the garlic cloves.

Add the octopus pieces to the salted water along with the onion, halved garlic clove, carrot, and bay leaf, and cook for approx. 45 minutes, until it is tender. Turn off the stove and leave the octopus to stand in the salted water for another 30 minutes. It is cooked when it can be picked up easily with a fork.

Peel the avocados and cut into cubes. Cut the tomatoes into quarters. Wash the parsley, pat dry, and chop finely. Squeeze the lemon and drizzle the juice over the avocados. Peel and finely chop the remaining garlic clove.

Remove the skin from the body of the octopus; it can stay on the tentacles. Cut the octopus into pieces and marinate with the chopped garlic, chili, rosemary, and olive oil.

Place the octopus pieces under a hot grill or in a grill pan and broil on each side for 2 to 3 minutes. Divide the tomatoes, avocados, and octopus between 4 plates and drizzle over the marinade. Season with salt and garnish with parsley.

Sweet potato soup with pepper Serves 4

3 sweet potatoes
2 shallots
2 tbsp coconut or olive oil
1 quart (1 liter) vegetable stock
juice of 1 lemon
4 tsp crème fraîche
1 tsp green pepper
1 tsp pink pepper
1½ tsp **SICHUAN PEPPER**
salt

Peel and roughly chop the sweet potatoes. Peel and chop the shallots.

Sauté the shallots in the oil in a large pot over medium heat until translucent. Add the sweet potato pieces and stir-fry for approx. 15 minutes.

Pour in the vegetable stock and bring everything to the boil, and then simmer over medium heat for about 15 minutes. Purée the soup using a handheld blender. Add lemon juice and salt to taste. Divide between 4 bowls and add a teaspoon of crème fraîche to each. Grind the 3 types of pepper together in a mortar and sprinkle over the soup.

Ajo Blanco Serves 4

Cut the bread into cubes, place in a bowl, and soak in a little milk for approx. 15 minutes. Peel and finely chop the garlic cloves.

Peel the cucumber. Squeeze out the bread and, using a food processor or a handheld blender, blend it to a smooth purée together with the almonds, garlic, olive oil, cucumber, and vinegar. Add a little water if necessary. Season with salt and pepper and leave to stand in the refrigerator for 1 hour.

Halve the melon, remove the seeds, scoop little balls out of the flesh, and place them in the refrigerator to chill. Before serving, strain the ajo blanco through a sieve. Serve with the melon balls and a few drops of olive oil.

4 slices (200 g) stale white bread
milk
4–5 medium-size **GARLIC CLOVES**
1 cucumber
2 cups (200 g) blanched almonds
generous ¾ cup (200 ml) olive oil
4 tbsp white wine vinegar
approx. 2 cups (500 ml) water
1 honeydew melon
salt, pepper

Pho Bo Serves 4

Bring the stock to the boil. Peel the ginger and shallots and chop them roughly. Crush the cardamom pods in a mortar and toast everything together with the cinnamon and star anise in a pan over medium heat until it begins to smell fragrant. Add the spices to the stock.

Add the fish sauce to the stock and simmer over low heat for approx. 45 minutes. Season to taste once again with salt and fish sauce.

Wash the herbs, shake them dry, and tear off the leaves. Chop everything finely. Wash the scallions and cut the green parts only into fine rings.

Cut the lime into eighths, slice the chili finely, and set it to one side along with the crushed pepper.

Bring a pot of water to the boil. Cook the noodles according to the packet instructions and divide between soup bowls.

Cut the raw fillet of beef against the grain into razor-thin slices, and place them on top of the noodles in each bowl.

Bring the stock back to the boil and pour it into the bowls when it is still boiling, so that all of the ingredients are equally covered. Scatter over the herbs and the mung bean sprouts, and serve the soup immediately with fish sauce, the lime quarters, the pepper, and the chili slices.

2 quarts (2 liters) beef stock
4-inch (10-cm) piece of **GINGER**
5 shallots
4 black cardamom pods
4 cinnamon sticks
4 star anises
3 tbsp fish sauce
salt
½ bunch of Vietnamese cilantro
½ bunch of long cilantro
½ bunch of Thai basil
1 bunch of scallions
1 lime
1 **CHILI**
black pepper, crushed
9 oz (250 g) rice noodles
11 oz (300 g) fillet of beef
2½ cups (200 g) mung bean sprouts

Ginger crème brûlée

For 4 ovenproof tins, each holding approx. 9 oz (250 ml)

1½-inch (4-cm) piece of GINGER
1 vanilla pod
generous 2 cups (500 g) cream
5 egg yolks
7 tbsp white sugar
4–5 tbsp brown sugar

Peel and finely chop the ginger. Slice the vanilla pod lengthways and scrape out the pulp. Put the cream, vanilla pulp, vanilla pod, and ginger in a pot and bring to the boil. Remove the pot from the heat and leave the ginger cream to stand for 30 minutes.

Pre-heat the oven to 210 °F (100 °C). Whisk the egg yolks and sugar using an egg whisk, then stir in the warm ginger cream, and strain everything through a fine-meshed sieve.

Divide the creamy mixture between the ovenproof tins. Bake in the oven for 45 to 60 minutes until firm. Remove the tins from the oven and leave to cool completely.

Shortly before serving, sprinkle brown sugar over the cream. Scorch with a flambé burner until the layer of sugar has caramelized. If required, sprinkle over another layer of sugar and caramelize it once again.

Chocolate mousse with Sichuan pepper

Serves 4

4 eggs
2 tbsp white sugar
2½ tbsp butter
2 cups (200 g) dark chocolate (60% cocoa), grated
½ tsp SICHUAN PEPPER

Separate the eggs. Beat the egg yolks with the sugar until they are frothy and the sugar has dissolved.

Melt the butter in a small pan. Chop the chocolate roughly, add to the butter, and stir it over low heat until it melts and the mixture is completely combined.

Crush the Sichuan pepper finely in a mortar and add it to the chocolate mixture. Beat the egg whites until they are semi-firm and gradually fold into the chocolate. Place the mousse in the fridge and leave for at least 4 hours.

Panna cotta with citrus fruit salad Serves 4

Put the cream and sugar in a pot and bring to the boil, then take it off the heat. Soak the gelatin in cold water, squeeze it out, and stir it into the hot cream.

Add the lemon peel to the cream. Leave to stand for 20 minutes, then strain through a fine-meshed sieve. Mix the cream with the yogurt and pour it into glasses. Chill in the refrigerator for at least 2 hours.

Peel and cut up the fruit with a sharp knife. Grind the pepper and sprinkle it over the fruit. Serve the fruit salad with the panna cotta.

generous 1½ cups (400 g) whipping cream
¾ cup + 2 tbsp (120 g) white sugar
2½ gelatin leaves
scant 1¼ cups (300 g) natural yogurt
grated peel of 1 lemon
2 grapefruits
1 blood orange
1 orange
1 lime
½ tsp **MOUNTAIN PEPPER**

Strawberry ice cream with Espelette pepper Serves 4

Wash and hull the strawberries and push them through a cap strainer. Add the confectioners' sugar and mix well.

In a second bowl, mix the whipping cream and mascarpone thoroughly with a handheld blender. Add the lemon juice, strawberry purée, and Espelette pepper, and mix everything thoroughly once more.

Pour the mixture into an ice cream maker and freeze according to the manufacturer's instructions. Alternatively, freeze for approx. 3 hours in the deep freezer.

The ice cream goes well with raspberry and rose crumble (see page 58).

5 cups (500 g) ripe strawberries
2½ cups (300 g) confectioners' sugar
1 cup (250 g) whipping cream
1 cup (250 g) mascarpone
3 tbsp lemon juice
pinch of **ESPELETTE PEPPER**

Exquisite, Finely Tuned Mixtures:

The Big Hitters

Some things are popular for a reason. Certain spice blends have been tried and tested for centuries, in North African, Middle Eastern, Indian, and European cuisine. Gingerbread seasoning, which lent an exotic note to the non-perishable baked treats that were popular in the Middle Ages, was not only flavorsome, but also healthy, thanks to its ingredients. Jewish, Lebanese, and Middle Eastern cuisine would be unthinkable without za'atar, while ras el hanout and dukkah enhance Arab and North African dishes. The spice blends garam masala and five-spice powder are essential to the Indian diet. But modern-day cuisine has moved on from 2,000 years ago, and so have spice mixtures. Nowadays, they impart flavors that unite different peoples and cultures. Spice blends are key to vegan cooking, fusion cuisine, and contemporary interpretations of classic recipes from all over the world. Most importantly, they are able to bring the big, wide world and all of its sensory associations into your kitchen.

Homemade Spice Mixtures

According to various diktats issued over the ages about the use of spices and seasonings, spice blends should consist solely of spices that are prepared according to their type or their purpose—in other words, blends such as goulash spices, spices for steak, or herbes de Provence. That said, you do not necessarily have to buy ready-packaged spices from the shops. Instead, you can make them yourself at home by putting in just a little effort. The good thing about this is that you can decide on the ingredients for yourself and adjust the proportion of each according to your own taste.

The following applies to the spice mixtures set out over the next few pages:

- The percentages given for the ratios of different spices within the mixture are only suggestions for your own basic blends. You can, of course, alter these quantities as you see fit.
- Unless otherwise indicated, all ingredients can be ground coarsely with a pestle and mortar or more finely in a standard spice or coffee grinder, according to taste.
- You can use standard kitchen bowls for mixing.
- Accurate digital kitchen scales are helpful for applying different quantities.

Five-spice powder

Five-spice powder is an Asian spice specialty that comprises the following ingredients:

equal parts:

cloves
star anise
Sichuan pepper
Chinese (Cassia) cinnamon
fennel seeds.

In an alternative version, the Sichuan pepper is replaced by ginger, and the fennel seeds by bay leaves. This spice blend goes very well with fish dishes and sauces.

Za'atar

Za'atar is a spice mixture that is particularly popular in Morocco and Tunisia. It is blended with olive oil and traditionally spread onto flatbreads before they are baked. It can also be used as a dip.

30% finely ground sumac
20% dried marjoram
10% dried oregano
10 % dried thyme

Mix together well, then add 20 percent toasted sesame seeds and 10 percent toasted pine nuts, and mix thoroughly once again. Stir together with olive oil until it forms a wet paste.

Dukkah

Dukkah is a traditional Egyptian spice mixture featuring hazelnuts and sesame seeds.

30% shredded hazelnuts, well toasted
30% golden brown, toasted sesame seeds
20% coriander seeds
10% cumin
10% black pepper

Mix everything together well and season to taste with coarse sea salt.

Curry powder

There are countless variations on this spice mixture, which is prevalent and popular within Indian cuisine. Here is an established basic recipe:

25% turmeric
15% cumin
15% coriander seeds
8% mustard seeds
6% sweet paprika
5% black pepper
4% ginger
3% Chinese (Cassia) cinnamon
3% bay leaves
3% grated nutmeg
2% chilies
2% cardamom
2% cloves
2% fenugreek seeds
2% lemongrass
2% allspice
1% Sichuan pepper

Garam masala

Garam masala is an Indian spice mixture that is ideal for seasoning Asian rice dishes. Here is a recipe that can be tweaked and supplemented according to taste:

35% coriander seeds
35% cumin
10% cardamom (ground in a bowl)
8% pepper
8% nutmeg
4% Chinese (Cassia) cinnamon

The easiest way to make this blend is to mix pre-ground spices. A more lavish method, but one that has a far more flavorsome end result, is to toast the whole individual spices briefly, and only then to grind them finely in a spice or coffee grinder.

Ras el Hanout

Anyone who has ever visited the spice dealers of the souks of Morocco will find themselves whisked back there by the beguiling scent of this blend. It is no mere coincidence that ras el hanout translates as "head of the spice emporium." As with curry powder, there are numerous recipes for ras el hanout, which vary from shop to shop, but here is an established recipe for the mixture:

25% cumin
15% turmeric
10% Chinese (Cassia) cinnamon
10% coriander seeds
5% aniseed
5% cloves
5% Java pepper
5% black pepper
5% nutmeg
5% ginger
3% chilies
2% allspice
2% bay leaves
2% lavender blossoms
1% cardamom seeds (ground without the pod)

This mixture can be prepared in a number of different ways. The simplest version is to buy all of the spices already ground, and then mix them thoroughly. A more elaborate and authentic way of doing it is to toast the whole spices briefly and then grind or shred them coarsely.

Ras el hanout is popular in traditional Moroccan couscous dishes and as a seasoning for chicken or grilled lamb!

Gingerbread spices

Once again, there are countless different versions of this spice mixture. Almost every traditional bakery has its own recipe, sometimes a carefully guarded secret. Here is an established and popular variant:

50% Chinese (Cassia) cinnamon
25% allspice
8% cloves
8% aniseed
5% cardamom
4% mace

This mixture not only gives gingerbread its distinctive flavor, but can also be used for other baked goods that are traditionally eaten at Christmas. It is often used in herbal teas, ice cream, and sorbets.

Spotlight on Spice Mixtures

For some, having different readymade spice mixtures on the kitchen shelf is indicative of a lack of creativity, while for others it is a veritable godsend. Indeed, there are plenty of good reasons to keep such blends at close hand—as long as they are good quality, of course.

But how can you gauge whether a spice mixture is good or not? The first, crucial pointer is the list of ingredients. "Seasoning mixes" may contain flavoring agents and additives such as cooking salt, starch, and lactose, alongside the spices themselves. This is not the case with proper spice mixtures.

Take note of the packaging, too. The bag or tin should be airtight and impermeable to light, ensuring that the spices retain their flavor for as long as possible. Avoid buying spice mixtures with packaging that features a transparent cellophane window. It might look cute, but it will have an impact on the quality. Before buying you should take a look at the expiration date; ideally, this will give the year in which the spices were harvested. The fresher the product, the more intense the flavor.

From a culinary point of view, it is worthwhile to invest in sustainably produced and carefully prepared spices. Ask a specialist retailer for advice—the difference in flavor will be ample reward for putting in the extra effort.

You can experiment with such blends as Café de Paris from Switzerland (used to flavor butter, which is then spread over grilled meat), berbere from Ethiopia, and ras el hanout from Morocco. Couscous, for instance, is traditionally made using ras el hanout, and the mixture can also give a distinctive, eastern flavor to barberry-studded rice with chicken. Berbere provides heat in Ethiopian cuisine; its main ingredients are ginger, garlic, cinnamon, coriander seeds, allspice, chili pepper, cloves, ajwain, and the dried fruits of the common rue plant.

Some spice mixtures include expensive and unusual spices that you simply would not buy individually, and which you may not even have heard of. Cajun spice blends are a good example: these fiery mixtures contain oregano, thyme, onion, garlic, and different sorts of chili, including cayenne, pequin, chipotle, and ancho, as well as black and white pepper.

The main advantage of readymade spice mixtures is that they can enhance the taste of certain dishes (not all are

suitable) with the wave of a hand, giving them a breadth of flavor—particularly useful if you are short of time. And those who prefer not to use readymade spice mixtures can make their own. Be creative! If you use the right packaging, your own creations could even make good gifts for friends. Especially if they then invite you to dinner …

Spotlight on Curry Powder

Curry powder is a spice mixture made from at least ten ingredients, and sometimes containing over twenty. Its uniform yellow color comes from turmeric. Making this mixture is something of an art, as the taste of no single spice can be allowed to overpower the rest. India is the birthplace of curry powder. Spice mixtures, known as masalas, have been in widespread use there for thousands of years. This local tradition later gave rise to curry powder. The origins of the curry mixtures prevalent today date back to the time of the British Raj in the 18th century. The colonial officials of that time were fascinated by Indian cuisine and were quick to copy the masalas that were most suited to their palate.

The British adopted the southern Indian word Kari, referring to various spicy dishes, and used it for the spice mixtures that were new to them. The word "curry" is derived from this stem. The new spice blends were soon adopted throughout Europe and won many fans across the whole of the British Empire. A number of spice-processing factories were founded in Madras in the late 18th century and exported curry blends all over the world.

Besides India, curry mixtures exist in other Asian countries such as Thailand, Sri Lanka, and Malaysia. These have very different components from the standard curry powder sold in shops in the West, but they still enjoy a long tradition within their respective regions of origin.

Salted cookies with za'atar Makes 20

3½ tbsp cold butter
¾ cup + 2 tbsp (120 g) flour
1 egg
3 tbsp ZA'ATAR
scant 6 tbsp (40 g) ground almonds
flour for the kitchen surface
salt

Cut the butter into small cubes, add to the flour together with the egg, salt, za'atar, and almonds, and mix everything briskly to form a smooth dough. Wrap the dough in plastic wrap and leave to stand in the refrigerator for 1 hour.

Pre-heat the oven to 390 °F (200 °C) and line a baking sheet with baking parchment. Roll the dough out on a lightly floured surface so that it is approx. 1/5 inch (5 mm) thick. Cut out cookie shapes or cut the dough into squares and bake for approx. 10 to 12 minutes.

Curry grissini Makes 40

2⅔ cups (400 g) durum wheat flour
scant ¾ cup (100 g) semolina
2 tbsp mild CURRY POWDER
1½ tsp (20 g) fresh yeast
1 tsp cane sugar
4 tbsp olive oil
2 tsp salt

Mix the flour, semolina, and curry powder in a bowl, and then make a well in the middle. Mix the yeast and sugar with 1¼ cups (300 ml) lukewarm water, pour into the well, and mix with a little flour. Cover the bowl and leave the mixture to prove in a warm place for 10 minutes.

Add the oil and knead everything for about 10 minutes to form a smooth, stretchy dough. Cover and leave the dough to prove in a warm place for approx. 1 hour, until it has visibly increased in volume.

Pre-heat the oven to 320 °F (160 °C). Divide the dough into 40 portions of equal size. Roll each portion out so that it is approx. ⅓ inch (8 mm) thick, and then cut them into strips, each also ⅓ inch (8 mm) thick. Place the dough strips on 2 baking sheets lined with baking parchment and leave to prove for approx. 15 minutes.

Bake the grissini in the oven for approx. 35 to 40 minutes, until golden brown, then remove them from the oven, leave to cool, and serve with hummus (see page 30) or other dips.

Feta with honey marinade and herbs Serves 4

Put the olive oil, honey, herbes de Provence, and vinegar in a small pot, bring the mixture to the boil, and then leave it to reduce until it is syrupy. Season with salt and pepper, remove from the heat, and leave to cool a little.

Wash the wild herbs and pat dry. Cut the chives into short lengths. Mix the herbs and chives together, and divide them between 4 plates.

Cut up the feta and scatter the pieces over the beds of salad. Drizzle generously with the honey vinaigrette, and garnish with the basil and cress.

This salad goes well with warm roasted vegetables or fresh pull-apart bread (see page 131)

2 tbsp olive oil
2 tbsp honey
1 tsp herbes de Provence or another herb mix
2–3 tbsp sherry vinegar or honey vinegar
1 handful of wild herb salad
½ bunch of chives
1 cup (150 g) feta
a few basil leaves
1 carton of cress
salt, white pepper

Spiced plum chutney Makes approx. 3 jars of 1 lb (450 ml) each

Wash and halve the plums and remove the pits, and chop the flesh roughly. Peel and finely chop the ginger and shallots. Wash the chili, slice it lengthways, and remove the seeds. Wash it once again and cut it diagonally into thin strips.

Put the shallots, ginger, chili, star anise, cinnamon, cloves, coriander seeds, cardamom, and pepper in a pot together with the honey and vinegar, and bring the mixture to the boil. Cover and simmer over low heat for 15 minutes.

Add the plum pieces and stew the fruit until the liquid has completely boiled off.

Rinse the jars out with boiling water, pour in the chutney, and seal the jars. Leave the chutney to stand for at least a week. It will keep in the refrigerator for about 3 months.

2¼ lb (1 kg) plums
1 oz (30 g) fresh ginger
4 shallots
1 red chili
3 star anises
1 cinnamon stick
2 cloves
1 tsp coriander seeds
2 crushed cardamom pods
½ tsp crushed peppercorns
⅓ cup (100 g) honey
7 tbsp Balsamic vinegar

Pull-apart bread with herb butter Serves 4

Mix the ingredients for the pre-dough together and leave to stand overnight at room temperature.

The next day, make the main dough by mixing the yeast, water, half the flour, salt, and sugar in a food processor on the lowest setting for 5 minutes, and then knead it on the second setting for 2 minutes.

Add the butter in pieces and knead on the second setting until it has been completely worked into the dough.

Add the rest of the flour and the eggs and continue to knead on the second setting for another 10 minutes, until you have a uniform-looking dough. Leave in a warm place for 2 hours to prove. The dough should double in volume.

Leave the dough overnight in the refrigerator so that it continues to rise.

Next day, chop the herbs using a kitchen mixer. Mix together the butter, garlic, herbs, and a teaspoon of salt, then set to one side.

Roll the dough out onto a lightly floured surface so that it is just ⅓ inch (1 cm) thick and spread it with the soft herb butter. Using a pastry wheel or a knife, cut it into squares with 3-inch (8-cm) sides.

Stack 5 to 6 squares of dough on top of one another and place them vertically in a greased loaf tin. Repeat this process until you have used up all of the squares of dough.

Leave to prove for another 2 hours. Pre-heat the oven to 355 °F (180 °C).

Bake the pull-apart bread for 40 minutes.

For the pre-dough
½ cup (75 g) wheat flour
⅓ cup (75 ml) water
1 g fresh yeast

For the main dough
5 g fresh yeast
1½ tbsp water
generous 1⅓ cups (200 g) wheat flour
1 tsp salt
1 tsp sugar
6 tbsp butter
2 eggs

For the filling
14 tbsp butter
1 bunch of mixed herbs: chervil, cress, parsley, pimpinella, sorrel, and chives
2 garlic cloves
Sea salt

Lamb burgers in ras el hanout rolls Serves 4

For the rolls

1⅔ cups (250 g) wheat flour
1½ tsp (20 g) fresh yeast
7 tbsp milk
1 tsp sugar
2 eggs
¾ oz (20 g) **RAS EL HANOUT**
7 tbsp butter
1 tsp salt
1 egg yolk
1 tbsp black sesame seeds

For the burgers

generous 1 lb (500 g) minced lamb
1 tsp harissa
generous ¾ cup (40 g) breadcrumbs
1 egg
2 tsp dried mint
salt
2 tbsp oil for frying
1 avocado
2 tomatoes
4 lettuce leaves
hummus (see page 30)

To make the burger rolls, mix together the flour, yeast, milk, and sugar, and leave to prove for 10 minutes.

Break the eggs and add them to the mixture along the with ras el hanout. Work in the cold butter and knead thoroughly for 10 minutes. Cover the dough and leave to prove at room temperature for 90 minutes.

Cut the dough into 4 pieces of equal size. Sprinkle each piece with flour and fold the edges into the middle with your fingers until you have a neat circle. Place the rolls on the kitchen surface and press them flat with the palm of your hand. Transfer them to a floured baking sheet, cover, and leave to prove for another 60 minutes.

Pre-heat the oven to 390 °F (200 °C). Brush the rolls with egg yolk and sprinkle with the sesame seeds. Bake in the oven for 20 minutes until golden brown.

Meanwhile, combine the meat with the harissa, breadcrumbs, egg, mint, and salt. Shape the mixture into 4 patties and fry them in a little oil in a hot pan for approx. 5 minutes on each side.

Halve the avocado and remove the pit. Cut it into slices, and sprinkle with a little salt. Wash and slice the tomatoes. Wash the lettuce leaves.

Cut each of the rolls in half and spread with a little hummus. Place one burger on each of the bottom halves of the rolls, and add avocado, tomato, and lettuce on top. Cover with the top halves of the rolls.

Persian saffron rice with barberries and chicken Serves 4

For the advieh

1 tsp black peppercorns
1 star anise
6 cardamom seeds
2 tsp coriander seeds
2 tsp dried rose petals
1 tsp ground cinnamon
1 tsp turmeric
½ grated nutmeg

For the chicken

1 cut-up chicken or 4 chicken thighs
3 tbsp clarified butter
2 garlic cloves
1 onion
2 tsp advieh
1 tsp salt
juice of 1 lemon
generous ¾ cup (200 ml) chicken stock
salt, pepper

For the rice

generous 1½ cups (300 g) Basmati rice
½ tsp saffron
2 cups (100 g) dried barberries
1 tbsp raw cane sugar
3½ tbsp + 1 tsp clarified butter
2 tbsp chopped pistachios

To make the spice mixture, grind the pepper, anise, cardamom, coriander seeds, and rose petals finely, and mix with the cinnamon, turmeric, and nutmeg.

Rinse the rice thoroughly. Bring to the boil in approx. 2 quarts (2 liters) water, simmer gently for 6 to 8 minutes, and then drain.

Crush the saffron in a mortar with a little sugar, then pour over some hot water to infuse. Wash the barberries thoroughly and add to a pan along with the sugar and 1 teaspoon of clarified butter. Leave them to caramelize slightly, and then set them aside.

Warm the rest of the clarified butter gently in a large pot, and then cover the bottom of the pot with rice. Pour in the saffron infusion and mix well with the rice, then add the rest of the rice to the pot.

Put the lid on the pot, wedging a tea towel in the top, and leave to cook over low heat for about an hour.

Meanwhile, fry the chicken pieces in the clarified butter. Peel and crush the garlic, and peel and halve the onion.

Add the onion, garlic, spices, lemon juice, and stock to the chicken. Cover and cook over low heat for 45 to 60 minutes. Season to taste with salt and pepper.

Remove the rice from the heat and place the pot in ice-cold water for 2 minutes, so that the crust comes away from the pot. Place a plate over the top of the pot and turn it quickly upside down so that the saffron crust is uppermost on the plate when the pot is removed. Sprinkle over the barberries and pistachios, and serve with the chicken.

Creamy polenta with spinach and poached eggs Serves 4

To make the dukkah, toast the almonds, hazelnuts, coriander seeds, cumin, and sesame seeds in a dry pan until they smell fragrant. Leave to cool and then grind coarsely in a kitchen mixer or mortar. Add and mix in the salt and pepper. Store any excess dukkah in an airtight container; its shelf life will depend on the expiry date of the nuts.

To make the polenta, bring the milk, stock, and a generous pinch of salt to the boil in a pot with high sides. Gradually add the polenta, stirring constantly. Bring to the boil once more over low heat, then remove it from the stove and stir in the butter and Gouda cheese.

Peel and finely chop the shallots and garlic. Wash the spinach and leave it to dry. Heat the oil in a pan and sauté the garlic and shallots over medium heat until they are translucent. Add the spinach and continue to cook for 3 to 4 minutes until it wilts. Grate in a little nutmeg, and season with salt and pepper.

Mix the vinegar into 1 quart (1 liter) of water and bring it to the boil. Crack the eggs carefully into a bowl, one by one, ensuring that the yolks remain intact. Stir the boiling vinegar water briskly with an egg whisk, then slide the eggs individually into the swirling liquid. The water should not be at boiling point any more. Remove the pot from the stove and leave the eggs to stand in the water for 3 to 4 minutes.

Remove the poached eggs with a slotted spoon and leave to dry. Divide the polenta between plates, add the spinach, and place the eggs on top. Scatter with the dukkah and serve.

For the dukkah
generous ⅓ cup (50 g) almonds
scant ½ cup (50 g) hazelnuts
1 tsp coriander seeds
1 tsp cumin
1 tbsp sesame seeds
½ tsp coarse sea salt
pinch of roughly ground black pepper

For the polenta
1¼ cups (300 ml) milk
2½ cups (600 ml) vegetable stock
salt
1 generous cup (200 g) polenta (cornmeal)
3 tbsp salted butter
7 tbsp grated Gouda cheese
2 shallots
1 garlic clove
7 cups (400 g) spinach, packed
3 tbsp olive oil
nutmeg
1 tsp vinegar
4 eggs (large)
salt, pepper

Fried merguez with fennel couscous Serves 4

For the merguez
3–4 chilies
2 garlic cloves
1 tbsp salt
2 tsp cumin
1 tsp paprika
20 peppercorns
2 tbsp olive oil
2¼ lb (1 kg) lamb belly or shoulder
(at least 20% fat)
intestines (ask your butcher)
4 tbsp oil

For the couscous
2 fennel bulbs
4 tbsp olive oil
juice of 1 orange
1 cup (200 g) couscous
½ bunch of parsley
salt

Using a food chopper, purée the chilies and garlic together with the salt, cumin, paprika, pepper, and olive oil until it forms a paste.

Cut the meat into cubes and mix with the paste. Leave it to chill, and then put it through a meat grinder.

Rinse the intestines in a bowl of water, so that a water bubble forms, then pull it over the spout of the sausage attachment on the meat grinder. Fill the intestinal tube with the meat, turning it to create 8 sausages.

To make the couscous, cut the fennel into thin strips. Heat 3 tablespoons of oil in a pan and fry the fennel for 4 minutes.

Add the orange juice to the fennel, and cook for another 4 to 5 minutes.

Bring 1 cup (250 ml) lightly salted water to the boil and gradually add the couscous. Add 1 tablespoon olive oil, remove the pot from the heat, cover it with a lid, and leave the couscous to stand for 8 minutes. Fluff up the couscous with a fork.

Fry the merguez sausages in the hot oil for 8 minutes, turning them often. Wash the parsley and shake it dry, then chop it and scatter it over the couscous along with the fennel. Serve with the merguez.

Pea and green curry soup Serves 4

Peel and finely chop the shallots, then fry them in the olive oil until translucent. Stir in the curry paste and fry gently, then pour in the stock and leave the mixture to simmer gently for 5 minutes.

Add the peas and leave to simmer for another 5 or 6 minutes. Wash the mint, shake it dry, and chop it roughly. Add it to the soup and purée everything with a handheld blender until it is smooth.

Strain the soup through a fine-meshed sieve, squeezing out any bits that are left. Stir in the cream and season the soup with salt and pepper.

2 shallots
2 tbsp olive oil
2 tsp green **CURRY PASTE**
1 quart (1 liter) vegetable stock
1 lb (500 g) frozen peas
1 bunch of fresh mint
scant 1 cup (100 g) whipping cream
salt, pepper

Lentil curry with mango and garam masala Serves 4

Peel and finely chop the garlic and ginger. Peel and chop the onion. Heat the coconut oil or butter in a pot and sauté the chili, ginger, garlic, and onion. Add the garam masala and cumin once the other ingredients are soft, and fry briefly.

Add the lentils, coconut milk, and tomatoes. Bring everything to the boil and simmer gently for 20 minutes. Season with salt.

Wash the parsley, shake it dry, and chop it finely. Peel the mango and cut it into cubes. Divide the curry between plates, scatter over the mango, and garnish with the parsley. Serve with fresh bread or Basmati rice.

1 garlic clove
¾ oz (20 g) ginger
1 onion
2 tbsp coconut oil or clarified butter
½ tsp chili flakes
1 tsp **GARAM MASALA**
1 tsp cumin
scant 1½ cups (300 g) yellow lentils
1¾ cups (400 g) coconut milk
14 oz (400 g) chopped tomatoes (can)
salt
½ bunch of parsley
1 mango

Moroccan chickpea salad Serves 4

generous 1 lb (500 g) baby carrots
3 tbsp olive oil
2 tsp RAS EL HANOUT
salt, pepper
2½ cups (400 g) precooked chickpeas
  (jar or can)
½ bunch of mint
1 lemon
1⅓ cups (200 g) feta

Pre-heat the oven to 390 °F (200 °C). Peel the carrots and slice them at an angle. Mix with 2 tablespoons of olive oil and 1 teaspoon of ras el hanout.

Place the carrot slices on a baking sheet lined with baking parchment. Season with salt and pepper, turn the slices so that they are well covered, and roast in the oven for 20 to 25 minutes.

Drain the chickpeas, rinse them under cold running water, then transfer them to a salad bowl. Tip the carrots and their oil over the chickpeas.

Tear the mint leaves from their stalks and chop them finely. Squeeze the lemon and mix the juice into the salad together with 1 teaspoon of ras el hanout and, if required, 1 extra tablespoon of olive oil. Season with salt and pepper. Crumble the feta and scatter over the salad.

Mussel soup with curry Serves 4

2 fennel bulbs
1 onion
4 cm piece of ginger
2 sticks of celery
2 tbsp butter
1 tbsp mild CURRY POWDER
generous ¾ cup (200 ml) white wine
1 cup (250 ml) fish stock
2⅓ lb (1 kg) mussels
¾ cup (200 g) whipping cream
salt, pepper
½ bunch of parsley

Remove the woody stalk from the fennel and cut it into small pieces. Peel the onion and ginger. Cut the celery and onion into strips and grate the ginger finely.

Heat the butter in a pot and sauté the onion until it is translucent. Add the ginger and curry powder. Pour in the white wine and bring to the boil, then add the fish stock. Leave the mixture to simmer, uncovered, for 15 minutes.

Meanwhile, clean the mussels, washing them thoroughly in cold water and discarding any that have opened. Bring a pot of salted water to the boil and cook the mussels for 8 minutes with the lid on.

Add the cream, mussels, fennel, and celery to the stock and cook for another 5 minutes with the lid off. Season with salt and pepper.

Wash the parsley, pat it dry, and then chop it. Divide the soup between bowls and garnish with the parsley. Serve with toasted French bread.

Carrot cake with orange blossom frosting
For 1 large cake tin

Pre-heat the oven to 355 °F (180 °C). To make the cake, peel and grate the carrots. Chop the hazelnuts roughly and toast them in a dry pan until they give off a nutty smell. Grease the cake tin.

Separate the eggs, and beat the egg yolks and butter until the mixture is frothy. Mix the flour, almonds, and baking powder thoroughly with the spices and orange peel. Gradually add the flour-and-spices mixture to the egg mixture.

Mix in the hazelnuts and grated carrots. Beat the sugar and egg whites with the salt in a kitchen mixer until they form stiff peaks. Fold them into the batter and pour everything into the greased cake tin. Bake for approx. 30 to 35 minutes, until a kitchen skewer comes out clean. Leave the cake to cool on a wire rack.

To make the frosting, mix the cream cheese and crème fraîche together with the orange blossom water, orange peel, and confectioners' sugar. Spread the cake with the frosting before serving.

For the cake
14 oz (400 g) carrots
⅔ cup (80 g) hazelnuts
4 eggs
14 tbsp butter or margarine at room
  temperature
generous 1⅓ cups (200 g) flour
1 cup (100 g) ground almonds
2 tsp baking powder
2 tsp cinnamon
½ tsp cardamom
½ tsp mace
½ tsp ground cloves
pinch of grated nutmeg
1 tsp ground ginger
grated peel of 1 orange
¾ cup + 2 tbsp (200 g) cane sugar
pinch of salt

For the frosting
⅔ cup (150 g) cream cheese
10 tbsp crème fraîche
1 tbsp orange blossom water
grated peel of ½ orange
1–2 level tbsp confectioners' sugar

Chai-affogato
Serves 4

Bring the water to the boil in a pot and add all of the spices. Simmer over low heat for 1 minute.

Add the tea, milk, and honey, and bring back to the boil, and then leave to stand for about 5 minutes.

Strain the chai through a sieve into 4 bowls or large cups. Add 1 scoop of vanilla ice cream to each and serve immediately.

6 cups of water
6 green cardamom pods
2 cloves
1 cinnamon stick
1 tsp aniseed
½ tsp ginger, finely chopped
4 tbsp strong black tea, e.g. Ceylon or Assam
4 cups of milk
6 tbsp honey or according to taste
4 scoops of vanilla ice cream

Index of Recipes

Ajo blanco 115

Avocado and chicken sandwich 30

Beet salad with goat's milk cheese 40

Bergamot pavlova with tangerine and lemon curd and persimmons 89

Braised leg of lamb with rosemary polenta 85

Buckwheat risotto with beet and scamorza 39

Burrata with cherries and pepper 107

Caraway and thyme crispbreads 33

Carrot and cardamom soup 82

Carrot cake with orange blossom frosting 143

Chai affogato 143

Chestnut soup with hazelnuts 39

Chicory and pear salad with dark rye bread croutons 81

Chocolate beet cake 44

Chocolate mousse with Sichuan pepper 116

Couscous salad with mushrooms 40

Creamy polenta with spinach and poached eggs 135

Cucumber yogurt with rose petals 57

Curry grissini 128

Duck rillettes à l'orange 81

Eggplant mousse 30

English scones with saffron 54

Fennel soup with star anise oil 82

Feta with honey marinade and herbs 129

Fillet of beef with chimichurri 108

Fish parcels with ginger 108

Fried merguez with fennel couscous 136

Fried zucchini flowers with lavender 57

Ginger crème brûlée 116

Gnocchi with melted tomatoes and star anise 86

Harissa 104

Hot salmon ceviche in coconut milk 107

Hummus 30

Lamb burgers in ras el hanout rolls 132

Lentil and goat's milk cheese salad with mustard dressing 111

Lentil curry with mango and garam masala 139

Mango and turmeric ice cream 43

Marinated salmon with orange and coriander 78

Melon gazpacho with rose petals 62

Moroccan chickpea salad 140

Mussel soup with curry 140

Orange and cardamom parfait 89

Orange blossom fougasse 54

Orange blossom tart 64

Oriental lamb casserole 34

Oven-baked seabream with lemongrass and zucchini 60

Panna cotta with citrus fruit salad 119

Pea and green curry soup 139

Persian saffron rice with barberries and chicken 134

Pho bo 115

Plantain chips 104

Poppy seed whirls 44

Pork tenderloin in orange caramel 85

Potato and sage pizza 84

Potato rösti with salmon tartare 33

Pull-apart bread with herb butter 131

Rabbit in tarragon and mustard sauce 111

Raspberry and rose crumble 58

Roasted almonds with smoked salt 33

Salted cookies with za'atar 128

Savory cheesecake 78

Spiced plum chutney 129

Spicy grilled octopus salad 112

Spicy olives 104

Spinach fritters with yogurt 34

Strawberry ice cream with Espelette pepper 119

Strawberry salad with roasted asparagus and vanilla vinaigrette 63

Sweet potato soup with pepper 112

Tomato soup with lemongrass 62

Tonka ice cream with hazelnut brittle 43

Vanilla and tomato jam 55

Vanilla flan 64

Vanilla risotto 61

Veal tenderloin with lavender glaze and blackberries 61

Warm roasted pepper salad with saffron 63

White asparagus tart with flower blossoms 58

Zucchini quiche with goat's milk cheese 86